CHESS
TARGET
PRACTICE

BATTLE TACTICS FOR EVERY
SQUARE ON THE BOARD

Bruce Pandolfini

A FIRESIDE BOOK
Published by Simon & Schuster
NEW YORK LONDON TORONTO SYDNEY TOKYO SINGAPORE

FIRESIDE
Rockefeller Center
1230 Avenue of the Americas
New York, New York 10020

Copyright © 1994 by Bruce Pandolfini

FIRESIDE and colophon are registered trademarks
of Simon & Schuster Inc.

Designed by Stanley S. Drate/Folio Graphics Co. Inc.
Manufactured in the United States of America

10   9   8   7   6   5   4   3   2

Library of Congress Cataloging-in-Publication Data
Pandolfini, Bruce.
     Chess target practice / Bruce Pandolfini.
          p.   cm.
     "A Fireside book."
     Includes index.
     ISBN 0-671-79500-7
     1. Chess.   2. Chess problems.   I. Title.
GV1449.5.P35   1994
794.1'2—dc20   94-2890
                                                           CIP

ISBN: 0-671-79500-7

For
Shelby Lyman

ACKNOWLEDGMENTS

I would like to thank Bruce Alberston, Idelle Pandolfini, Carol Ann Caronia, Nick Viorst, Deirdre Hare, Burt Hochberg, and my editor, Kara Leverte, for their valuable efforts.

I would also like to thank Larry Tamarkin for producing the diagrams with Chess Base.

Contents

Introduction

There are two traditional ways to study tactics: randomly, approximating the conditions of real games; and conceptually, using categories such as "pins" and "forks." Both of these schemes, random and thematic, are valid and useful, and sometimes they're even offered in the same book.

Chess Target Practice combines these methods with a twist. As in actual play, motifs are unrelated from example to example, but, if you like, you can analyze them by theme using the Tactical Index in the Appendix. In this special new presentation they are also organized by square.

For example, under "a1," you will encounter several winning attacks that typically occur when an enemy unit moves to that square. Such an arrangement stresses the importance of the board itself. Moreover, by focusing on definite locations, you give yourself reference points to reinforce the concept. Learn these standard associations and you'll have a stockpile of weapons to draw upon for quick kills in your own games.

The format is simple. Each example is presented under the name of a specific square. The names are arranged by file, starting with the a-file and ending with the h-file. Each example is numbered, diagramed, and given in chess notation for verification and further practice in recognizing squares.

Various classifications appear with each example. Under **ENEMY MOVE** you will find the losing player's last move. Usually a signpost that a mistake has taken place, it is always a move to the square given at the top of the page. Following is the **PRIMARY TARGET** and, in some cases, a **SECONDARY TARGET**. The primary target is the square occupied by the chief object of attack. The secondary target, if any, is generally a square occupied by a lesser enemy unit, but it might simply be a transitional square used by an attacking unit to reach a destination square and complete a stratagem. If a couple of units seem to qualify as a target, the order of precedence is king first, then queen, rook, bishop, knight, and pawn. If targets are given equal weight, they are separated by a slash, with the more important one coming first.

The **BATTLE TACTIC** is the stratagem that achieves the winning position. The **RESPONSE** is the main winning line, given no more than three moves deep, without the defender's replies. The **RESULT** gives the anticipated outcome. The **ATTACK PROFILE** presents an overview, explaining the situation in words, while the **OBSERVATION** offers a related comment.

You can take advantage of *Chess Target Practice* in several ways. Certainly read it from start to finish, examining each diagram and trying to guess the targets, battle tactics, and winning moves. Or turn to it for study of specific themes, as listed in the Tactical Index. You might even want to keep it nearby as a handbook, looking up specific squares as they interest you in your own games. However you employ it, I hope you find it as much fun as I did putting it together.

Algebraic Notation

You can get more from this book if you understand algebraic notation, which is a way to record moves using letters and numbers. To start with, view the chessboard as an eight-by-eight grid. Every square on the grid has its own name, derived from the connecting files and ranks. Files, the lines of squares going up and down, are lettered *a* through *h*. Ranks, the lines of squares going across, are numbered *1* through *8*. Squares are designated by combining a letter, printed lowercase, followed by a number. Thus, in the starting position, White's queen occupies *d1* and Black's queen occupies *d8*. All squares in the algebraic system are named from White's side. The algebraic grid given below indicates the names of all the squares. You may find it helpful to photocopy the grid and use it as a bookmark, so it's always there for review.

The algebraic grid. Every square has a unique name.

a8	b8	c8	d8	e8	f8	g8	h8
a7	b7	c7	d7	e7	f7	g7	h7
a6	b6	c6	d6	e6	f6	g6	h6
a5	b5	c5	d5	e5	f5	g5	h5
a4	b4	c4	d4	e4	f4	g4	h4
a3	b3	c3	d3	e3	f3	g3	h3
a2	b2	c2	d2	e2	f2	g2	h2
a1	b1	c1	d1	e1	f1	g1	h1

Other Symbols

You will find it useful to learn the following symbols:

SYMBOL	MEANING
K	king
Q	queen
R	rook
B	bishop
N	knight
—	moves to
x	captures
+	check
+ +	checkmate
0-0	castles kingside
0-0-0	castles queenside

Note that pawns are not identified by a symbol in game scores. If no indication of the moving unit is given, it must be a pawn.

The Shortest Chess Game

The shortest possible chess game consists of two moves for White and two for Black, with Black winning by checkmate. It is diagramed here, with each illustration's corresponding move appearing underneath.

1. f3
White moves the pawn on f2 to f3.

1. . . . e5
Black moves the pawn on e7 to e5.

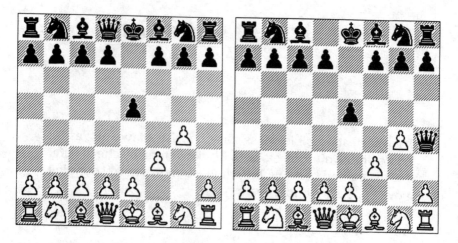

2. g4
White moves the pawn on g2 to g4.

2. . . . Qh4 + +
Black moves the queen on d8 to h4,
giving checkmate.

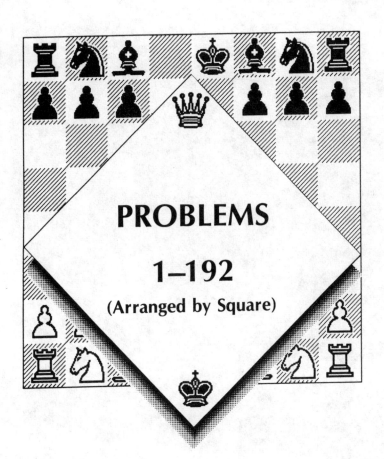

PROBLEMS

1–192

(Arranged by Square)

1

POSITION: W: Kg1 Be1 Nb1 Pa2 Pc4 Pe4 Pf3 (7)
B: Kg8 Be7 Na1 Pa7 Pc5 Pe5 Pf6 (7)

WHITE
TO MOVE

ENEMY MOVE:	1. . . . Nc2xa1
PRIMARY TARGET:	a1
SECONDARY TARGET:	None
BATTLE TACTIC:	Trapping
RESPONSE:	2. Na3 3. Bc3 4. Bxa1
RESULT:	White gains a knight (1–0).
ATTACK PROFILE:	Black's knight is threatening to escape at c2. It's stymied by guarding c2 and eliminated by direct attack.
OBSERVATION:	A clumsy knight can be trapped and won.

POSITION: W: Kd1 Pa2 Pb2 (3)
B: Kd8 Na1 (2)

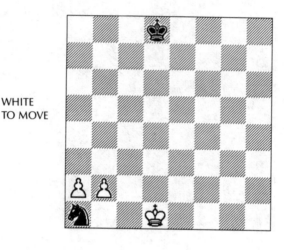

WHITE
TO MOVE

ENEMY MOVE:	**1. . . . Nc2xa1**
PRIMARY TARGET:	a1
SECONDARY TARGET:	None
BATTLE TACTIC:	Trapping
RESPONSE:	**2. Kc1 3. Kb1 4. Kxa1**
RESULT:	White wins the pawn ending (1–0).
ATTACK PROFILE:	Already frustrating the knight's flight, the king simply moves over, attacks it, and captures it.
OBSERVATION:	A king can do its own dirty work.

POSITION: W: Kb4 Qd2 (2)
B: Kb1 Qa1 (2)

WHITE
TO MOVE

ENEMY MOVE:	**1. . . . a2-a1(Q)**
PRIMARY TARGET:	b1
SECONDARY TARGET:	None
BATTLE TACTIC:	Mating net
RESPONSE:	**2. Kb3**
RESULT:	Black is soon mated (1–0).
ATTACK PROFILE:	This situation happens typically after White wins a pawn race. Black's last move was to make a new queen, but even this can't ward off mate.
OBSERVATION:	Don't count on a cornered queen.

21

POSITION: W: Kc1 Pb2 Pc2 (3)
B: Kf8 Ba2 (2)

WHITE
TO MOVE

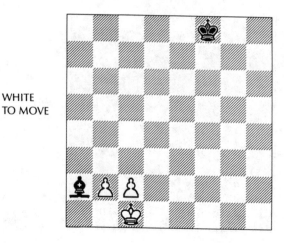

ENEMY MOVE:	**1. . . . Be6xa2**
PRIMARY TARGET:	a2
SECONDARY TARGET:	None
BATTLE TACTIC:	Trapping
RESPONSE:	**2. b3 3. Kb2 4. Kxa2**
RESULT:	White wins the bishop (1–0).
ATTACK PROFILE:	White blocks the bishop's escape with the b-pawn and snares it with the king. Black could get a pawn for the bishop, but White would eventually make a new queen.
OBSERVATION:	Eat a rook pawn at your own risk.

POSITION: W: Ke1 Qd1 Nf3 Pb2 Pc3 Pg2 (6)
B: Ke8 Qd8 Na2 Pd5 Pe6 Pf7 (6)

WHITE
TO MOVE

ENEMY MOVE:	1. . . . Nb4xa2
PRIMARY TARGET:	e8
SECONDARY TARGET:	a2
BATTLE TACTIC:	Fork
RESPONSE:	2. Qa4+ 3. Qxa2
RESULT:	White gains a knight (1–0).
ATTACK PROFILE:	Black's capture on a2 leaves the knight without a safe exit. A queen fork at a4 picks off the intruder.
OBSERVATION:	If you can't get out, don't go in.

POSITION: W: Kd2 Rf1 Bf2 Pb3 Pc2 (5)
B: Kf7 Qa2 (2)

WHITE
TO MOVE

ENEMY MOVE:	**1. . . . Qa3xa2**
PRIMARY TARGET:	a2
SECONDARY TARGET:	None
BATTLE TACTIC:	Trapping
RESPONSE:	**2. Bd4 + 3. Ra1**
RESULT:	White wins the queen for a rook (1–0).
ATTACK PROFILE:	Black thinks there's time to take the a-pawn and get out next move. But a discovered check stops the queen's escape, and the rook ropes it.
OBSERVATION:	Losing time by pawn-grabbing can lose big-time.

POSITION: W: Ke1 Qd1 Ba3 Nb1 Pd4 Pf2 (6)
B: Ke8 Qd8 Be7 Bc6 Pd5 Pf7 (6)

BLACK
TO MOVE

ENEMY MOVE:	1. Bc1-a3
PRIMARY TARGET:	a3
SECONDARY TARGT:	e1
BATTLE TACTIC:	Fork
RESPONSE:	1. . . . Bxa3 2. . . . Qa5 + 3. . . . Qxa3
RESULT:	Black gains a piece (0–1).
ATTACK PROFILE:	For the fork to work, Black must trade bishops on a3 first, then check with the queen at a5. If Black checks first, White saves the day by blocking at d2 with the queen.
OBSERVATION:	Play the right moves, in the right order.

POSITION: W: Kg1 Qe1 Rb1 Nc3 Pf2 Pg2 (6)
B: Ke8 Qa3 Ra8 Nc6 Pa7 Pe7 (6)

WHITE
TO MOVE

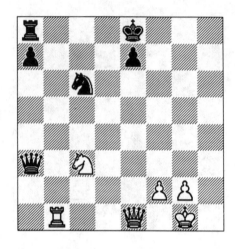

ENEMY MOVE:	**1. . . . Qa5xa3**
PRIMARY TARGET:	a3
SECONDARY TARGET:	c7
BATTLE TACTIC:	Double threat
RESPONSE:	**2. Nb5 3. Nc7 + 4. Nxa8**
RESULT:	White wins a rook (1–0).
ATTACK PROFILE:	The knight gives a double attack from b5, menacing the queen and a forking check at c7, a square the queen once guarded. Black saves the queen but loses the rook.
OBSERVATION:	It can't guard the square if it's no longer there.

POSITION: W: Kb1 Bc1 Nc3 Pa3 Pb2 Pc2 (6)
B: Kg8 Bb4 Nc4 Pb7 Pf7 Pg7 (6)

BLACK
TO MOVE

ENEMY MOVE:	1. a2-a3
PRIMARY TARGET:	a3
SECONDARY TARGET:	c3
BATTLE TACTIC:	Removing the guard
RESPONSE:	1. . . . Nxa3 + 2. . . . Bxc3
RESULT:	Black wins at least a pawn (0–1).
ATTACK PROFILE:	The b-pawn is overloaded, guarding both a3 and c3. Black's knight takes on a3 with check. If White takes back, his knight falls to the bishop. If instead the king moves out of check, Black's knight captures another pawn.
OBSERVATION:	If under attack, avoid pushing pawns in front of your castled king.

POSITION: W: Kd3 Ba4 Pa2 Pb2 Pc2 (5)
B: Kd7 Nc6 Pa6 Pb7 Pc5 (5)

BLACK
TO MOVE

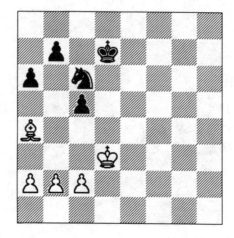

ENEMY MOVE:	**1. Bb5-a4**
PRIMARY TARGET:	a4
SECONDARY TARGET:	d3
BATTLE TACTIC:	Trapping
RESPONSE:	**1. . . . b5 2. . . . c4 +**
RESULT:	Black wins a bishop for a pawn (0–1).
ATTACK PROFILE:	White should have traded bishop for knight (1. Bxc6 +). Instead he kept the pin and now loses the bishop. Trying to get two pawns for the piece (3. Bxc4) fails to 3. . . . Ne5 +.
OBSERVATION:	Retreat if you must, but not into a blind alley.

11

POSITION: W: Kd1 Na4 Pa2 Pd3 (4)
B: Kc6 Ba3 Pb7 Pd4 (4)

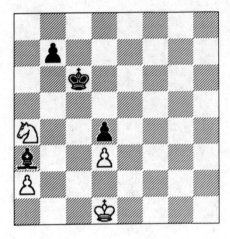

BLACK
TO MOVE

ENEMY MOVE:	1. Nc3-a4
PRIMARY TARGET:	a4
SECONDARY TARGET:	None
BATTLE TACTIC:	Trapping
RESPONSE:	1. . . . b5 2. . . . bxa4
RESULT:	Black wins a knight (0–1).
ATTACK PROFILE:	White blunders by placing the knight on the board's edge, where it has limited mobility. A direct pawn thrust wins the steed, for it hasn't a safe move.
OBSERVATION:	A rim knight is a slim knight.

POSITION: W: Ke1 Qd2 Bf1 Nd5 Pf2 (5)
      B: Ke8 Qa4 Be7 Nf6 Pd6 (5)

WHITE
TO MOVE

ENEMY MOVE:	**1. . . . Qd7xa4**
PRIMARY TARGET:	e8
SECONDARY TARGETS:	a4/b5
BATTLE TACTIC:	Fork
RESPONSE:	**2. Bb5 + 3. Nc7 + 4. Nxb5**
RESULT:	White wins the queen for a bishop (1–0).
ATTACK PROFILE:	White draws the queen to an exploitable square by a forking check with the bishop. The knight then forks king and queen, and the queen is won. All is lost.
OBSERVATION:	Putting king and queen in the same line is a no-no.

POSITION: W: Kg1 Qd1 Bc4 Pc3 Pd4 Pg2 (6)
B: Kg8 Qd8 Na5 Pc7 Pf7 Pg7 (6)

WHITE
TO MOVE

ENEMY MOVE:	**1. . . . Nc6-a5**
PRIMARY TARGET:	f7
SECONDARY TARGET:	a5
BATTLE TACTIC:	Fork
RESPONSE:	**2. Bxf7+ 3. Qh5+ 4. Qxa5**
RESULT:	White gains a pawn (1–0).
ATTACK PROFILE:	Black removed the knight from the center just to attack the bishop. White capitalizes by taking the f-pawn with check, which draws out Black's king. White's queen then forks at h5, regaining the piece (the knight at a5).
OBSERVATION:	A lone knight on the edge can fall off.

POSITION: W: Ke1 Qd1 Be2 Nd4 Pb2 Pc3 Pf2 (7)
B: Ke8 Qe7 Ba5 Nb8 Pb7 Pf7 (6)

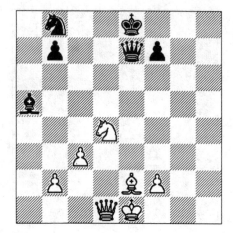

WHITE
TO MOVE

ENEMY MOVE:	**1. . . . Bb4-a5**
PRIMARY TARGET:	e8
SECONDARY TARGET:	a5
BATTLE TACTIC:	Fork
RESPONSE:	**2. Qa4+ 3. Nxc6 4. Qxa5**
RESULT:	White wins a piece (1–0).
ATTACK PROFILE:	Black should have moved his bishop to c5 or d6. On a5, it falls to a queen check at a4. If Black's knight defends at c6, White trades knights and then takes the bishop.
OBSERVATION:	Loose pieces are lost pieces.

POSITION: W: Kf1 Qd1 Bc4 Pb2 Pc3 Pf2 (6)
B: Kf8 Qd8 Ba5 Pc7 Pd6 Pf7 (6)

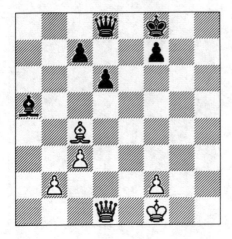

WHITE
TO MOVE

ENEMY MOVE:	**1. . . . Bb4-a5**
PRIMARY TARGET:	f7
SECONDARY TARGET:	a5
BATTLE TACTIC:	Double threat
RESPONSE:	**2. Qd5 3. Qxa5**
RESULT:	White wins a bishop (1–0).
ATTACK PROFILE:	On the previous move, Black had two possible retreats for his bishop. He chose the losing one, withdrawing to a5. By moving the queen to d5, White threatens mate at f7 and the bishop. The bishop goes.
OBSERVATION:	If one move loses, and one doesn't, play the one that doesn't.

POSITION: W: Kg1 Be4 Nd2 Pa3 Pb2 Pe3 Pg2 (7)
B: Kg8 Na5 Na6 Pb7 Ph7 (5)

WHITE
TO MOVE

ENEMY MOVE:	1. . . . Nb8-a6
PRMARY TARGET:	a5
SECONDARY TARGETS:	a6/c6
BATTLE TACTIC:	Fork
RESPONSE:	2. b4 3. b5
RESULT:	White wins a knight for a pawn (1–0).
ATTACK PROFILE:	Black's knights are poorly positioned on the edge of the board. White starts by attacking the a5-knight. Its only safe square is c6, but retreating there allows a further advance, forking both knights. One of them is atomized.
OBSERVATION:	Badly placed knights are sadly chased knights.

POSITION:　W: Ke1 Ra1 Be5 Nb5 Pb2 Pe2 (6)
　　　　　　 B: Ke8 Ra8 Bc8 Na6 Pa7 Pb7 (6)

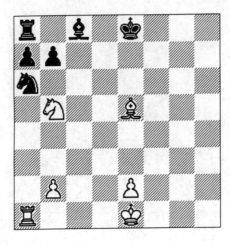

WHITE
TO MOVE

ENEMY MOVE:	1. . . . Nb8-a6
PRIMARY TARGET:	a6
SECONDARY TARGET:	a8/e8
BATTLE TACTIC:	Fork
RESPONSE:	2. Rxa6 3. Nc7 + 4. Nxa8
RESULT:	White wins a knight (1–0).
ATTACK PROFILE:	Black tried to guard c7 by developing his knight to a6. But the knight can be removed, and with it Black's hopes of avoiding material loss. If Black recaptures on a6, White's knight checks at c7. This regains the sacrificed rook and leaves White a piece ahead.
OBSERVATION:	Don't pin your hopes on a removable object.

POSITION: W: Kg1 Ba6 Pd3 Pf2 Pg2 Ph2 (6)
B: Kh8 Rc8 Pc5 Pg7 (4)

BLACK
TO MOVE

ENEMY MOVE:	**1. Bc4xa6**
PRIMARY TARGET:	a6
SECONARY TARGET:	a1
BATTLE TACTIC:	Pin
RESPONSE:	**1. . . . Ra8 2. . . . Rxa6**
RESULT:	Black wins the bishop (0–1).
ATTACK PROFILE:	Black is driven to save his attacked rook, which he does by pinning the bishop. If the bishop moves, White is mated on the first rank.
OBSERVATION:	Even if you're losing, you can still play the best defense.

POSITION: W: Kg1 Ra5 Ba7 Pf3 Pg2 (5)
B: Kg8 Ra8 Be7 Pf7 Pg7 (5)

BLACK
TO MOVE

ENEMY MOVE:	**1. Be3xa7**
PRIMARY TARGET:	a7
SECONDARY TARGET:	g1
BATTLE TACTIC:	Fork
RESPONSE:	**1. . . . Rxa7 2. . . . Bc5 + 3. . . . Bxa7**
RESULT:	Black wins a bishop (0–1).
ATTACK PROFILE:	White captured a pawn on a7 with the wrong piece. Black wins the bishop by sacrificing his rook. If White takes back, Black regains the rook by a bishop check at c5.
OBSERVATION:	Take with the one you don't need to keep.

POSITION: W: Kb2 Ba7 Pb3 Pd4 (4)
B: Kb5 Nd7 Pb7 Pd5 (4)

BLACK
TO MOVE

ENEMY MOVE:	**1. Bb8xa7**
PRIMARY TARGET:	a7
SECONDARY TARGET:	None
BATTLE TACTIC:	Trapping
RESPONSE:	**1. . . . b6 2. . . . Ka6 3. . . . Kxa7**
RESULT:	Black picks up the bishop (0–1).
ATTACK PROFILE:	Black allowed White to capture on a7, knowing there's no exit. Then the b-pawn shuts the door at b6, and the king retreats to chomp the bishop. White can get a pawn for the bishop, but that's it.
OBSERVATION:	If the enemy lets you do it, don't.

21

POSITION: W: Kg2 Rh8 (2)
               B: Kf7 Ra7 (2)

WHITE
TO MOVE

ENEMY MOVE:	**1. . . . Ra6xa7**
PRIMARY TARGET:	f7
SECONDARY TARGET:	a7
BATTLE TACTIC:	Skewer
RESPONSE:	**2. Rh7 + 3. Rxa7**
RESULT:	White wins a rook and soon mates (1–0).
ATTACK PROFILE:	This is a standard endgame trick. Black's rook took the pawn on a7 before it reached the last rank to promote. White checks on the seventh rank, skewering king and rook. The king must move out of the way and the rook is seized.
OBSERVATION:	Seize the 7th rank and watch what happens.

POSITION: W: Kb1 Rd1 Bf3 Na7 Pa2 Pb2 Pc2 (7)
B: Ke8 Ra8 Bg7 Nf6 Pb7 Pc6 (6)

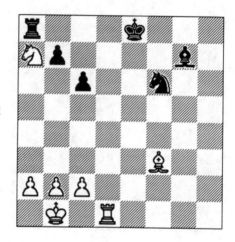

WHITE
TO MOVE

ENEMY MOVE:	**1. . . . Rb8-a8**
PRIMARY TARGET:	c6
SECONDARY TARGETS:	e8/a8
BATTLE TACTIC:	Fork
RESPONSE:	**2. Nxc6 3. Bxc6+ 4. Bxa8**
RESULTS:	White wins at least a pawn (1–0).
ATTACK PROFILE:	Black thinks White's knight is trapped beyond the front lines. He overlooks an annihilating sacrifice on c6 and a follow-up bishop fork on the same square, pilfering the rook on a8. So the knight breaks through with a free capture of the c6-pawn.
OBSERVATION:	Few barriers are impenetrable.

POSITION: W: Kf2 Be3 Na8 Pd4 (4)
B: Kd7 Nf5 Pb5 Pd5 Pe4 (5)

BLACK
TO MOVE

ENEMY MOVE:	**1. Nc7xa8**
PRIMARY TARGET:	e3
SECONDARY TARGET:	a8
BATTLE TACTIC:	Trapping
RESPONSE:	**1. . . . Nxe3 2. . . . Kc6 3. . . . Kb7**
RESULT:	Black wins the pawn ending (0–1).
ATTACK PROFILE:	White's knight is trapped. First Black simplifies, exchanging knight for bishop. After White takes back on e3, Black's king snares the interloper, moving from d7 to c6 to b7 to a8. Black's passed pawns will then decide the outcome.
OBSERVATION:	If two pawns up, swap down.

POSITION: W: Kg1 Ra7 Bg2 Pd4 (4)
B: Kg8 Rd8 Ba8 Pd5 (4)

WHITE
TO MOVE

ENEMY MOVE:	**1. . . . Bb7-a8**
PRIMARY TARGET:	a8
SECONDARY TARGETS:	d5/g8
BATTLE TACTIC:	Fork
RESPONSE:	**2. Rxa8 3. Bxd5 + 4. Bxa8**
RESULT:	White clears the board and wins (1–0).
ATTACK PROFILE:	Black tried to safeguard the bishop by moving it to a8, but that loses to a temporary sacrifice, destroying d5's protection. Black's rook retakes on a8, the bishop demolishes d5, and Black has nothing left. White easily makes a new queen.
OBSERVATION:	A dead defender can't defend.

25

POSITION: W: Ke3 Ne2 Pa2 Pb3 Pf4 (5)
B: Kf7 Bb1 Pa7 Pb6 Pf5 (5)

WHITE
TO MOVE

ENEMY MOVE:	1. . . . Bd3-b1
PRIMARY TARGET:	b1
SECONDARY TARGET:	None
BATTLE TACTIC:	Trapping
RESPONSE:	2. Nc3 3. Kd2 4. Nxe4
RESULT:	White forces a winning trade (1–0).
ATTACK PROFILE:	Black's bishop, trying to attack White's pawns, gets encircled. At c3 the knight attacks the bishop and defends the pawn. The bishop goes to c2, the king attacks it, and a trade results on e4. White wins the pawn ending.
OBSERVATION:	Bishops move on diagonals. Open ones.

POSITION: W: Ke1 Rb1 Bd3 Nc3 Pb2 Pf3 (6)
B: Kg8 Rb8 Bg7 Nc6 Pf7 Pg6 (6)

BLACK
TO MOVE

ENEMY MOVE:	**1. Ra1-b1**
PRIMARY TARGET:	b2
SECONDARY TARGETS:	c3/e1
BATTLE TACTIC:	Fork
RESPONSE:	**1. . . . Rxb2 2. . . . Bxc3 +**
RESULT:	Black wins at least a pawn (0–1).
ATTACK PROFILE:	Responding to Black's aggressive rook, White passively protected the b-pawn with his own rook. Black undermines c3 by sacrificing on b2. White retakes, but loses the knight with check. After 3. Rd2 Nd4, Black regains the exchange and another pawn to boot.
OBSERVATION:	Activate your rook, deactivate your opponent's.

POSITION: W: Kb1 Rg1 Bg2 Nd5 Pb2 Pc2 (6)
B: Kh8 Ra8 Bf5 Nc5 Ph6 (5)

BLACK
TO MOVE

ENEMY MOVE:	**1. Kc1-b1**
PRIMARY TARGET:	b1
SECONDARY TARGET:	None
BATTLE TACTIC:	Mating net
RESPONSE:	**1. . . . Nb3 2. . . . Ra1**
RESULT:	Black forces mate (0–1).
ATTACK PROFILE:	White stopped the rook from penetrating to a1. But moving the king to b1 has put the c-pawn in a pin, allowing Black's knight to invade at b3. The knight, safe from capture, insures the very intrusion White wanted to prevent.
OBSERVATION:	It's hard to flee what you run toward.

POSITION: W: Kg1 Qd1 Ra1 Be2 Nc3 Pa3 Pd4 Pf2 (8)

B: Kg8 Qb2 Rf8 Bb7 Nf6 Pd5 Pg7 (7)

WHITE
TO MOVE

ENEMY MOVE:	**1. . . . Qb6xb2**
PRIMARY TARGET:	b2
SECONDARY TARGET:	None
BATTLE TACTIC:	Trapping
RESPONSE:	**2. Na4**
RESULT:	White wins the queen for a rook (1–0).
ATTACK PROFILE:	Black's queen has taken the poisoned b-pawn. The knight attacks the queen and the square b6, the only possible escape. Black can cut his loss by surrendering queen for rook.
OBSERVATION:	The b-pawn can cause indigestion.

POSITION: W: Kg1 Ra1 Ba2 Nc3 Pc2 Pf2 (6)
B: Kf7 Rb2 Bd7 Nf6 Pe6 (5)

WHITE
TO MOVE

ENEMY MOVE:	**1. . . . Rb8xb2**
PRIMARY TARGET:	b2
SECONDARY TARGET:	None
BATTLE TACTIC:	Trapping
RESPONSE:	**2. Bb3 3. Nd1**
RESULT:	White wins the exchange (1–0).
ATTACK PROFILE:	Black pays for taking the b-pawn. The bishop blocks the Black rook's departure by moving to b3. The rook will be forced to offer itself for the bishop once the knight attacks it.
OBSERVATION:	It's not what you take, but what you keep.

POSITION: W: Kg2 Bb2 Nc3 Pb3 Pe4 (5)
B: Kb7 Bg7 Nf6 Pd6 Pe7 (5)

BLACK
TO MOVE

ENEMY MOVE:	**1. Bc1-b2**
PRIMARY TARGET:	e4
SECONDARY TARGETS:	c3/b2
BATTLE TACTIC:	Pin
RESPONSE:	**1. . . . Nxe4**
RESULT:	Black wins a pawn (0–1).
ATTACK PROFILE:	Developing to b2, White has put his bishop in a precarious line. Black's capture of the e4-pawn uncovers a pin along the a1-h8 diagonal. If White takes the knight, Black munches the bishop. Black's connected pawns then insure a winning endgame.
OBSERVATION:	Don't pin your own pieces.

31

W: Ke2 Bb3 Nd4 Pa2 Pb2 Pf3 (6)
B: Kg7 Bd7 Nf6 Pb5 Pc7 Pf7 (6)

BLACK
TO MOVE

ENEMY MOVE:	**1. Bd5-b3**
PRIMARY TARGET:	d4
SECONDARY TARGET:	b3
BATTLE TACTIC:	Trapping
RESPONSE:	**1. . . . c5 2. . . . c4**
RESULT:	Black wins a piece for a pawn (0–1).
ATTACK PROFILE:	The first move with the c-pawn drives White's knight to c2, closing off the bishop's escape. The second advance, to c4, traps the bishop. White gets only a pawn for the piece.
OBSERVATION:	A thrusting pawn can cut two pieces.

POSITION: W: Kc1 Rd3 Be2 Pe3 (4)
B: Kg8 Rb8 Nb3 Pc7 (4)

WHITE
TO MOVE

ENEMY MOVE:	1. . . . Na5xb3 +
PRIMARY TARGET:	b3
SECONDARY TARGET:	g8
BATTLE TACTIC:	Fork
RESPONSE:	2. Rxb3 3. Bc4 + 4. Bxb3
RESULT:	White wins a knight (1–0).

ATTACK PROFILE: Black has taken on b3 with the wrong piece. The knight gives check, but White, by sacrificing rook for knight, follows with a forking check at c4, winning a piece. Instead of starting with the knight, Black should have reversed the order, first capturing on b3 with the rook.

OBSERVATION: In a two-move sequence, occasionally play the second move first.

33

POSITION: W: Kh1 Ra2 Rg1 Pb2 Pd4 Ph2 (6)
B: Kh8 Qb3 Pa4 Pd5 (4)

WHITE
TO MOVE

ENEMY MOVE:	1. . . . Qb5-b3
PRIMARY TARGET:	b3
SECONDARY TARGET:	h3
BATTLE TACTIC:	Pin
RESPONSE:	2. Ra3 3. Rh3 + +
RESULT:	Black must give up the queen (1–0).
ATTACK PROFILE:	Black snipes at White's rook. Forced to defend it, White moves it to menace the queen. The rook also threatens mate at h3 once her majesty moves to safety. Black must sacrifice the queen for the rook to avoid sudden death.
OBSERVATION:	The hunted also knows how to hunt.

POSITION: W: Kf3 Nc3 Pa2 Pd4 Pe4 (5)
B: Kg8 Nd7 Pb4 Pc7 (4)

WHITE
TO MOVE

ENEMY MOVE:	**1. . . . b5-b4**
PRIMARY TARGETS:	b4/c7
SECONDARY TARGET:	None
BATTLE TACTIC:	Fork
RESPONSE:	**2. Nd5**
RESULT:	White wins a pawn (1–0).
ATTACK PROFILE:	Black's advance of the b-pawn is weakening and overextensive. White exploits this by jumping his knight to d5, forking pawns at b4 and c7. One of these two is obliterated.
OBSERVATION:	Push them. Don't rush them.

POSITION: W: Ke1 Qd1 Nf3 Pd5 Pe4 (5)
B: Ke8 Qd8 Nb4 Pd6 Pe5 (5)

WHITE
TO MOVE

ENEMY MOVE:	**1. . . . Nc6-b4**
PRIMARY TARGET:	e8
SECONDART TARGET:	b4
BATTLE TACTIC:	Fork
RESPONSE:	**2. Qa4 + 3. Qxb4**
RESULT:	White wins a knight (1–0).
ATTACK PROFILE:	Black moved the knight to b4 to escape White's prickly d5-pawn (retreating to e7 would have been more prudent). A queen check at a4 refutes the incursion.
OBSERVATION:	Crossing the frontier can be perilous.

POSITION: W: Kg1 Qd1 Ra1 Bc1 Pa4 Pf2 Pg2 (7)
B: Kg8 Qb4 Rf8 Bc8 Pf7 Pg7 (6)

WHITE
TO MOVE

ENEMY MOVE:	**1. . . . Qe7xb4**
PRIMARY TARGET:	b4
SECONDARY TARGET:	f8
BATTLE TACTIC:	Skewer
RESPONSE:	**2. Ba3 3. Bxf8**
RESULT:	White wins the exchange (1–0).
ATTACK PROFILE:	White has an indirect defense of b4, which Black didn't see. From a3, White's bishop can skewer Black's queen and rook. After the queen moves to safety, White takes the rook. The price? A mere bishop.
OBSERVATION:	Undetected doesn't mean unprotected.

37

POSITION: W: Ke1 Ra1 Bc4 Pb3 Pc2 Pe4 (6)
B: Ke8 Ra8 Bc8 Pa6 Pb5 (5)

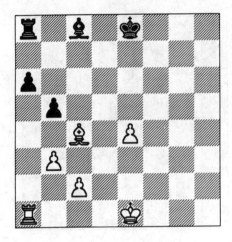

WHITE
TO MOVE

ENEMY MOVE:	1. . . . b7-b5
PRIMARY TARGET:	b5
SECONDARY TARGET:	a8
BATTLE TACTIC:	Pin
RESPONSE:	2. Bxb5 +
RESULT:	White wins a pawn (1–0).
ATTACK PROFILE:	Black advanced the pawn to b5 to attack the bishop. But White's bishop can seize the b-pawn because its defender, the a-pawn, is pinned. If it takes on b5, White's rook captures Black's.
OBSERVATION:	If it's in a pin, you can win.

POSITION: W: Ke1 Bb5 Pc2 Pf3 (4)
B: Ke8 Nc6 Pd7 Pe5 Pf7 (5)

BLACK
TO MOVE

ENEMY MOVE:	**1. Bf1-b5**
PRIMARY TARGET:	b5
SECONDARY TARGETS:	c2/f3
BATTLE TACTIC:	Fork
RESPONSE:	**1. . . . Nd4**
RESULT:	Black wins a pawn (0–1).
ATTACK PROFILE:	The bishop attacks the knight, but since it's not a pin, the knight turns it around and attacks the bishop. The bishop can be salvaged, but one of White's pawns must be junked.
OBSERVATION:	Retaliate. If it attacks you, attack it.

39

POSITION: W: Kg1 Qd1 Bb5 Pf3 Pg2 (5)
B: Kg8 Qd8 Nc6 Pd6 Pf7 Pg7 (6)

BLACK
TO MOVE

ENEMY MOVE:	**1. Bd3-b5**
PRIMARY TARGET:	g1
SECONDARY TARGET:	b5
BATTLE TACTIC:	Fork
RESPONSE:	**1. . . . Qb6 + 2. . . . Qxb5**
RESULT:	Black wins the bishop (0–1).
ATTACK PROFILE:	Since the a7-g1 diagonal is open, shifting the bishop to b5 was a blunder, punished by a queen check at b6. White can get out of check, but can't rescue the bishop.
OBSERVATION:	Check to avoid checks.

POSITION: W: Kg1 Qe2 Rf1 Bb1 Pb2 Pf2 Pg2 (7)
B: Kg8 Qf8 Ra8 Bc8 Pa7 Pb6 Pf7 Pg7 (8)

WHITE
TO MOVE

ENEMY MOVE:	**1. . . . b7-b6**
PRIMARY TARGET:	g8
SECONDARY TARGET:	a8
BATTLE TACTIC:	Double threat
RESPONSE:	**2. Qe4**
RESULT:	White wins at least a bishop (1–0).
ATTACK PROFILE:	Black has moved the b-pawn to flank his bishop, when it could have been developed at once. White penalizes this faulty logic by a queen move that threatens mate and the rook at a8. Black must move the bishop to f5, sacrificing it to avoid even greater loss.
OBSERVATION:	Don't prepare when you can just do.

POSITION: W: Kg1 Qd1 Bg3 Pa4 Pd4 Pf2 (6)
B: Ke8 Qf7 Bb6 Pa7 Pc7 Pd5 (6)

WHITE
TO MOVE

ENEMY MOVE:	**1. . . . Bc5-b6**
PRIMARY TARGET:	b6
SECONDARY TARGETS:	e8/a5
BATTLE TACTIC:	Fork
RESPONSE:	**2. a5 3. Qa4 +**
RESULT:	White wins a bishop for a pawn (1–0).
ATTACK PROFILE:	Black's bishop retreated to a losing square, and the a-pawn attacks it. After the pawn is taken, White's queen has a winning fork at a4.
OBSERVATION:	A retreat isn't always a vacation.

POSITION: W: Kg1 Qd1 Be3 Nd4 Pb2 Pe4 Pf3 Pg4 (8)

B: Ke8 Qb6 Bg7 Nf6 Pd7 Pe6 Pf7 (7)

WHITE
TO MOVE

ENEMY MOVE:	1. . . . Qd8-b6
PRIMARY TARGET:	b6
SECONDARY TARGET:	g7
BATTLE TACTIC:	Discovery
RESPONSE:	2. Nf5 3. Nxg7 +
RESULT:	White wins a bishop (1–0).
ATTACK PROFILE:	To attack a pawn Black dared to put his queen on the same diagonal as White's bishop. This allows a bishop discovery on Black's queen when the knight moves to f5. After the queen moves, Black's bishop is captured for free.
OBSERVATION:	Only a fool looks down a loaded gun barrel.

43

POSITION: W: Kh2 Qc2 Bg2 Nf3 Pf2 Pg3 Ph4 (7)
B: Kg8 Qd8 Bb7 Bf8 Pf7 Pg7 Ph7 (7)

WHITE
TO MOVE

ENEMY MOVE:	**1. . . . Bc8-b7**
PRIMARY TARGET:	g8
SECONDARY TARGET:	b7
BATTLE TACTIC:	Double threat
RESPONSE:	**2. Ng5 3. Bxb7**
RESULT:	White wins a bishop (1–0).
ATTACK PROFILE:	Black developed his bishop to an undefended square (b7). White uncovers an attack on it by threatening mate at h7. Since the mate threat must be dealt with, the unprotected bishop is lost.
OBSERVATION:	Really ask for it and you'll get it.

POSITION: W: Kg1 Qe2 Nf3 Pd5 Pf2 Pg2 (6)
B: Ke8 Qd8 Bb7 Pc7 Pd6 Pe5 (6)

WHITE
TO MOVE

ENEMY MOVE:	**1. . . . Bc8-b7**
PRIMARY TARGET:	e8
SECONDARY TARGET:	b7
BATTLE TACTIC:	Fork
RESPONSE:	**2. Qb5 + 3. Qxb7**
RESULT:	White wins the bishop (1–0).
ATTACK PROFILE:	Black's bishop, undefended at b7, attacks a pawn. Black's king is vulnerable along the a4-e8 diagonal. The connection point is b5. White's queen goes there and wins the bishop.
OBSERVATION:	If the king is on an open line, secure the line or get it off.

POSITION: W: Ke1 Qb7 Rh1 Nd2 Ng1 Pe3 Pg2
Ph2 (8)

B: Kg8 Qd8 Ra8 Bd7 Nb8 Pa7 Pf7 Pg7
(8)

BLACK
TO MOVE

ENEMY MOVE:	1. Qb3xb7
PRIMARY TARGET:	b7
SECONDARY TARGETS:	g2/h1
BATTLE TACTIC:	Fork
RESPONSE:	1. . . . Bc6 2. . . . Bxg2 3. . . . Bxh1
RESULT:	Black wins at least a rook (0–1).
ATTACK PROFILE:	White goes pawn hunting and threatens the rook at a8. Black's bishop counters by seizing the a8-h1 diagonal. After the queen moves to safety, Black cleans up, taking the pawn at g2 and the rook at h1.
OBSERVATION:	Suddenly, the defender can be the attacker.

POSITION: W: Kc1 Qd2 Be3 Bf3 Pb2 Pc3 Pg2 (7)
B: Kg8 Qc7 Rb8 Bc8 Pa7 Pb6 Pf7 (7)

WHITE
TO MOVE

ENEMY MOVE:		**1. . . . Ra8-b8**
PRIMARY TARGET:		c7
SECONDARY TARGET:		b8
BATTLE TACTIC:		Skewer
RESPONSE:		**2. Bf4**
RESULT:		White wins a rook (1–0).
ATTACK PROFILE:		Black's rook is a sitting duck at b8. White shoots it with a skewer from f4. After the queen moves off the b8-h2 diagonal, the rook is plucked.
OBSERVATION:		Rooks don't do diagonals.

POSITION: W: Kc3 Nb8 Pb4 Pd4 (4)
 B: Kd8 Bd7 Pd5 Pe6 (4)

BLACK
TO MOVE

ENEMY MOVE:	**1. Na6-b8**
PRIMARY TARGET:	b8
SECONDARY TARGET:	None
BATTLE TACTIC:	Trapping
RESPONSE:	**1. . . . Bb5 2. . . . Kc7**
RESULT:	Black wins a full knight (0–1).
ATTACK PROFILE:	From b8 the knight hopes to capture the bishop or escape at a6. Shifting the bishop to b5 frustrates both possibilities. Black's king simply sidles over and captures the knight.
OBSERVATION:	On the border, you might as well take the knight off.

POSITION: W: Kc2 Rh1 Nd5 Pb3 Pc4 Pg2 (6)
B: Kg8 Rb8 Bc5 Pa7 Pc7 Pf7 (6)

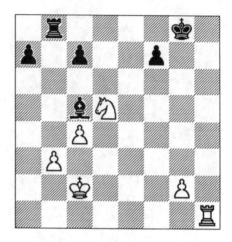

WHITE
TO MOVE

ENEMY MOVE:	**1. . . . Ra8-b8**
PRIMARY TARGET:	b8
SECONDARY TARGET:	c5
BATTLE TACTIC:	Fork
RESPONSE:	**2. Nf6 + 3. Nd7 4. Nxc5**
RESULT:	Black loses the bishop (1–0).
ATTACK PROFILE:	White can capture the pawn at c7, but it's better to fork rook and bishop from d7. By first checking on f6, the knight gains time to reach d7 before Black can defend. To save the rook Black must abandon the bishop.
OBSERVATION:	If you can't do it, first check and *then* do it.

POSITION: W: Kg3 Qb4 (2)
B: Kc1 Pc2 (2)

WHITE
TO MOVE

ENEMY MOVE:	**1. . . . Kb1-c1**
PRIMARY TARGET:	c1
SECONDARY TARGET:	None
BATTLE TACTIC:	Mating net
RESPONSE:	**2. Kf2 3. Qe1+ +**
RESULT:	Black is mated (1–0).
ATTACK PROFILE:	Instead of stepping on the a-file, Black's king stumbled in front of the pawn. White's king comes over to guard e1, preparing mate on that square.
OBSERVATION:	A blocked pawn can't queen on the next move.

50

POSITION: W: Ke1 Qe3 Rc1 Nc3 Pd4 Pg3 (6)
B: Kh7 Qc7 Rc8 Bg7 Pg6 Ph5 (6)

BLACK
TO MOVE

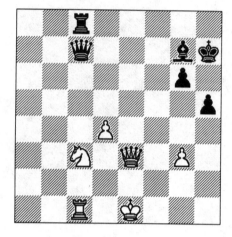

ENEMY MOVE:	1. Ra1-c1
PRIMARY TARGET:	e3
SECONDARY TARGET:	c1
BATTLE TACTIC:	Skewer
RESPONSE:	1. . . . Bh6 2. . . . Bxc1
RESULT:	Black wins a rook (0–1).
ATTACK PROFILE:	In defending the knight, White placed his rook on the same diagonal as his queen. The two are skewered from h6. The queen moves out of attack and the bishop takes the rook for nothing.
OBSERVATION:	Better to move it and keep it than to guard it and lose it.

POSITION: W: Kf2 Rc1 Re2 Pb3 Pc2 (5)
B: Kg8 Rc3 Rc8 Pa5 Pb4 Pf7 Pg6 (7)

BLACK
TO MOVE

ENEMY MOVE:	**1. Rf1-c1**
PRIMARY TARGET:	b3
SECONDARY TARGET:	c1
BATTLE TACTIC:	Pin
RESPONSE:	**1. . . . Rxb3**
RESULT:	Black wins a pawn (0–1).
ATTACK PROFILE:	White defends c2, but that puts the c-pawn in a pin. So Black's rook captures on b3. If the c-pawn takes the rook, Black takes White's rook at c1. Rooks are traded and Black gains a pawn.
OBSERVATION:	Protecting a man doesn't necessarily prevent its capture.

69

POSITION: W: Kg1 Qf4 Rd1 Bd2 Pf2 Pg2 (6)
B: Kg8 Qc2 Rc8 Nf6 Pf7 Pg7 (6)

WHITE
TO MOVE

ENEMY MOVE:	**1. . . . Qc7xc2**
PRIMARY TARGET:	c2
SECONDARY TARGET:	c8
BATTLE TACTIC:	Skewer
RESPONSE:	**2. Rc1 3. Rxc8 +**
RESULT:	White wins a lot of material (1–0).
ATTACK PROFILE:	Black's queen avoided a trade and instead took a pawn, threatening White's rook. The attacked unit becomes the attacker by moving to c1. Black has the unenviable choice of sacrificing his queen for the rook or moving the queen off the c-file, losing the rook at c8.
OBSERVATION:	Trading and taking are better than taking and losing.

POSITION: W: Kg1 Re1 Bf1 (3)
B: Kg8 Rc2 Bf3 Pf7 Pg7 (5)

WHITE
TO MOVE

ENEMY MOVE:	1. . . . Rc8xc2
PRIMARY TARGET:	h7
SECONDARY TARGET:	c2
BATTLE TACTIC:	Fork
RESPONSE:	2. Re8+ 3. Bd3+
RESULT:	White wins a rook (1–0).
ATTACK PROFILE:	Black took a pawn on c2. White checks on the last rank, forcing Black's king to h7. A forking bishop check at d3 pilfers Black's invasive marauder.
OBSERVATION:	A check can upset the best-laid rooks.

POSITION: W: Kg1 Qc2 Re2 Bd3 Pc3 Pd4 Pg2 (7)
B: Kh8 Qd8 Rc8 Nc6 Pd5 Pg7 Ph7 (7)

BLACK
TO MOVE

ENEMY MOVE:	1. Qd1-c2
PRIMARY TARGET:	d4
SECONDARY TARGETS:	c2/e2
BATTLE TACTIC:	Pin
RESPONSE:	1. ... Nxd4 2. ... Nxe2 +
RESULT:	Black wins the exchange and a pawn (0–1).
ATTACK PROFILE:	In attacking h7, White developed the queen to the same file as Black's rook. Thus Black's knight can take on d4 without fear of being captured, for the c-pawn shielding the queen is pinned. The knight next captures on e2, gaining the exchange.
OBSERVATION:	Attack, but expect counterattack.

W: Kg1 Qd1 Bd3 Pc2 Pf2 Pg3 (7)
B: Kg8 Qf8 Bc3 Pg7 Ph7 (6)

WHITE
TO MOVE

ENEMY MOVE:	1. . . . Bf6xc3
PRIMARY TARGET:	h7
SECONDARY TARGET:	c3
BATTLE TACTIC:	Fork
RESPONSE:	2. Bxh7 + 3. Qd3 +
RESULT:	White wins a pawn (1–0).
ATTACK PROFILE:	White sacrifices his bishop, taking a pawn with check. If the king takes back, White's queen forks king and bishop from d3.
OBSERVATION:	Opposite-color bishops are not always a big draw.

POSITION: W: Kc1 Qg1 Rd1 Nc3 Pb2 Pc2 Pg3 (7)
B: Kg8 Qc7 Rc8 Ne6 Pb5 Pf7 Pg7 (7)

BLACK
TO MOVE

ENEMY MOVE:	**1. Ne2-c3**
PRIMARY TARGET:	c3
SECONDARY TARGET:	c2
BATTLE TACTIC:	Pin
RESPONSE:	**1. . . . b4 2. . . . bxc3**
RESULT:	Black wins the knight for a pawn (0–1).
ATTACK PROFILE:	White's knight is pinned, shielding against Black's mate threat at c2. Black wins the pinned knight by attacking it with the b-pawn.
OBSERVATION:	If it's pinned, push and win.

POSITION: W: Kc1 Qe2 Rd1 Nd2 Pb2 Pc3 (6)
B: Kc8 Qc6 Bf5 Bf8 Pb7 Pc7 (6)

BLACK
TO MOVE

ENEMY MOVE:	**1. c2-c3**
PRIMARY TARGET:	c1
SECONDARY TARGET:	None
BATTLE TACTIC:	Mating net
RESPONSE:	**1. . . . Qxc3 + 2. . . . Ba3 + +**
RESULT:	Black forces mate (0–1).
ATTACK PROFILE:	White's queenside pawn weaknesses enable Black to force mate. First the queen is sacrificed on c3 with check. After it's taken, Black's dark-square bishop mates on a3.
OBSERVATION:	Some pawn moves are weak. All are permanent.

POSITION: W: Kg1 Qd1 Be3 Pd4 Pf2 Pg2 (6)
B: Ke8 Qd8 Nc4 Pd6 Pe7 Pf7 (6)

WHITE
TO MOVE

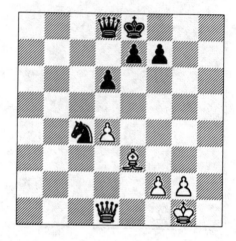

ENEMY MOVE:	**1. . . . Nb6xc4**
PRIMARY TARGET:	e8
SECONDARY TARGET:	c4
BATTLE TACTIC:	Fork
RESPONSE:	**2. Qa4 + 3. Qxc4**
RESULT:	White wins the knight (1–0).
ATTACK PROFILE:	Black's knight is overextended and susceptible. Though White does not directly hit c4, he has an indirect defense. The knight is picked off by a forking queen check at a4.
OBSERVATION:	The best defenses are those your opponent can't see.

59

POSITION: W: Kg1 Rc4 Rf1 Nf3 Pg2 (5)
            B: Kg8 Ra8 Rf8 Bc8 Pf6 Pg7 (6)

BLACK
TO MOVE

ENEMY MOVE:	**1. Rc1xc4**
PRIMARY TARGET:	c4
SECONDARY TARGET:	f1
BATTLE TACTIC:	Skewer
RESPONSE:	**1. . . . Ba6**
RESULT:	Black wins the exchange (0–1).
ATTACK PROFILE:	White's rooks occupy the same a6-f1 diagonal. Black's bishop slides to a6, insuring the gain of a rook for a bishop.
OBSERVATION:	Bishops can put a slant on rooks.

POSITION: W: Kg1 Bc4 Ne4 Pd4 Pf2 (5)
B: Kg8 Bd7 Be7 Pd6 Pe6 Pf7 (6)

BLACK
TO MOVE

ENEMY MOVE:	**1. Bd3xc4**
PRIMARY TARGETS:	c4/e4
SECONDARY TARGET:	None
BATTLE TACTIC:	Fork
RESPONSE:	**1. . . . d5**
RESULT:	Black wins a piece for a pawn (0–1).
ATTACK PROFILE:	White's bishop captured on c4, exposing both his bishop and his knight to attack. So the d-pawn advances, forking both of White's minor pieces. The knight can flail at c5, but the bishop whips it off, and Black emerges a piece ahead.
OBSERVATION:	Watch your step. Some squares are mined.

61

POSITION: W: Kg1 Qd1 Bd4 Pf4 Pg2 (5)
B: Ke8 Qb6 Bc5 Pf6 Pg7 (5)

WHITE
TO MOVE

ENEMY MOVE:	**1. . . . Bf8-c5**
PRIMARY TARGET:	e8
SECONDARY TARGET:	c5
BATTLE TACTIC:	Fork
RESPONSE:	**2. Qh5 + 3. Qxc5**
RESULT:	White wins a bishop (1–0).
ATTACK PROFILE:	If Black's king is on its original square, his f-pawn has moved to f6, and the fifth rank is clear, then developing the f8-bishop to c5 exposes it to a queen check at h5. All of this actually happens.
OBSERVATION:	So it shall be written, so it shall be done.

POSITION: W: Kg1 Qd1 Be3 Nd4 Pf2 Pg2 Ph3 (7)
B: Ke8 Qd8 Bc5 Nc6 Pd7 Pf7 (6)

WHITE
TO MOVE

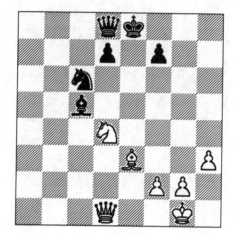

ENEMY MOVE:	1. . . . Bf8-c5
PRIMARY TARGET:	c6
SECONDARY TARGET:	c5
BATTLE TACTIC:	Discovery
RESPONSE:	2. Nxc6 3. Qxd8+ 4. Bxc5
RESULT:	White wins a piece (1–0).
ATTACK PROFILE:	Black placed his bishop in jeopardy by developing it to c5. By moving his knight, White can unveil an attack, bishop to bishop. So White trades knights and queens and then takes the bishop for free.
OBSERVATION:	Upon winning a piece, clear the board of all unneeded pieces.

63

POSITION: W: Ke1 Qd1 Nc5 Pe3 Pf2 (5)
B: Kg8 Qd8 Nf6 Pd7 Pg7 (5)

BLACK
TO MOVE

ENEMY MOVE:	1. Nb3xc5
PRIMARY TARGET:	e1
SECONDARY TARGET:	c5
BATTLE TACTIC:	Fork
RESPONSE:	1. . . . Qa5 + 2. . . . Qxc5
RESULT:	Black wins the knight (0–1).
ATTACK PROFILE:	White's knight capture on c5 allows a winning queen fork. After White gets out of check, Black takes the knight for nothing.
OBSERVATION:	An unanchored knight could drift away.

POSITION: W: Kg2 Rc1 Bb5 Pa4 Pf4 Pg3 (6)
B: Ke8 Ra8 Bf6 Pb7 Pc6 (5)

WHITE
TO MOVE

ENEMY MOVE:	1. . . . c7-c6
PRIMARY TARGET:	c6
SECONDARY TARGETS:	e8/a8
BATTLE TACTIC:	Fork
RESPONSE:	2. Rxc6 3. Bxc6 +
RESULT:	White wins two pawns (1–0).
ATTACK PROFILE:	Ordinarily, the best way to block a bishop check at b5 is with the c-pawn. This usually gains time by counterattacking the bishop. But here the rook simply takes it. If Black takes back, White's bishop captures on c6 with check, usurping the rook in the corner.
OBSERVATION:	Nothing is safe against the sac.

POSITION: W: Ke1 Bb5 Pd4 Pe3 (4)
B: Ke8 Nc6 Pb7 Pc7 (4)

WHITE
TO MOVE

ENEMY MOVE:	**1. . . . Nb8-c6**
PRIMARY TARGET:	c6
SECONDARY TARGET:	e8
BATTLE TACTIC:	Pin
RESPONSE:	**2. d5 3. dxc6**
RESULT:	White wins a knight for a pawn (1–0).
ATTACK PROFILE:	White checked on b5, and Black answered by putting his knight in a pin on c6. Since the knight cannot move, White wins by advancing the pawn to d5. The knight is captured next move.
OBSERVATION:	To block a bishop check, stick a pawn in its face.

66

POSITION: W: Kg2 Qc6 Nf3 Pc3 Pg3 (5)
B: Ke8 Qb8 Bc8 Nc5 Pb6 Pe6 (6)

BLACK
TO MOVE

ENEMY MOVE:	1. Qa4xc6 +
PRIMARY TARGET:	c6
SECONDARY TARGET:	None
BATTLE TACTIC:	Trapping
RESPONSE:	1. . . . Bd7
RESULT:	White loses the queen for a piece (0–1).
ATTACK PROFILE:	Black's knight chased White's queen from a4. The queen took the c-pawn with check, but at c6 there is no escape. The bishop blocks the check at d7 and the queen is lost.
OBSERVATION:	Enter, but leave the door open behind you.

POSITION: W: Kh1 Qe3 Rc1 Nc3 Pd4 Pf2 Ph2 (7)
B: Ke8 Qc7 Rb8 Bd6 Pc6 Pd5 Pe4 (7)

WHITE
TO MOVE

ENEMY MOVE:	**1. . . . Qd8-c7**
PRIMARY TARGET:	d5
SECONDARY TARGET:	c7
BATTLE TACTIC:	Pin
RESPONSE:	**2. Nxd5 3. Qxe4 +**
RESULT:	White wins two pawns (1–0).
ATTACK PROFILE:	Black threatens the h-pawn and a skewer at f4. Unfortunately, White's knight captures the d-pawn for free, since the c-pawn is pinned by White's rook. Black's e-pawn falls a move later.
OBSERVATION:	Keep your eyes open to avoid having them closed.

POSITION: W: Kh1 Qd1 Nc3 Nd4 Pa2 Pg2 Ph2 (7)
B: Ke8 Qc7 Bd6 Bc8 Pa6 Pb5 Pf7 (7)

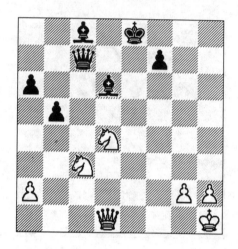

WHITE
TO MOVE

ENEMY MOVE:	**1. . . . Qd8-c7**
PRIMARY TARGET:	b5
SECONDARY TARGETS:	c7/d6
BATTLE TACTIC:	Fork
RESPONSE:	**2. Ndxb5 3. Nxb5 4. Nxd6 +**
RESULT:	White wins two pawns (1–0).
ATTACK PROFILE:	Black is attacking in two directions: along the c-file and the b8-h2 diagonal. But in so doing his queen is exposed. By virtue of a clever sacrifice on b5, White ends up winning two pawns.
OBSERVATION:	A threat can backfire in its own execution.

POSITION: W: Kg1 Rc7 Nf3 Pf2 Pg2 (5)
B: Kg8 Rd8 Be7 Pb7 Pg7 (5)

BLACK
TO MOVE

ENEMY MOVE:	**1. Rc1-c7**
PRIMARY TARGET:	h2
SECONDARY TARGET:	c7
BATTLE TACTIC:	Fork
RESPONSE:	**1. . . . Rd1 + 2. . . . Bd6 + 3. . . . Bxc7**
RESULT:	Black wins a rook (0–1).
ATTACK PROFILE:	White's rook went to the seventh rank, giving a double attack but abandoning the home rank. That allows a rook check at d1 and a bishop fork at d6, gaining tthe intrusive rook.
OBSERVATION:	For a rook, there's no place like home rank.

POSITION: W: Kh2 Qd2 Rc1 Bg2 Pc4 Pf4 Pg3 (7)
B: Kg8 Qe6 Rc8 Bf6 Pf7 Pg6 (6)

WHITE
TO MOVE

ENEMY MOVE:	**1. . . . Rf8-c8**
PRIMARY TARGET:	e6
SECONARY TARGET:	c8
BATTLE TACTIC:	Skewer
RESPONSE:	**2. Bh3 3. Bxc8**
RESULT:	White wins the exchange (1–0).
ATTACK PROFILE:	In ganging up on the c-pawn, Black placed his rook on the same diagonal as his queen. The two are sliced by a bishop's skewer from h3, which gains rook for bishop.
OBSERVATTION:	Rooks belong on open files and closed diagonals.

POSITION: W: Kg1 Rc1 Nd5 Pe4 Pg2 (5)
                 B: Kg8 Rc8 Nc6 Pe5 Pg7 (5)

WHITE
TO MOVE

ENEMY MOVE:	**1. . . . Rf8-c8**
PRIMARY TARGET:	c6
SECONDARY TARGET:	g8
BATTLE TACTIC:	Fork
RESPONSE:	**2. Rxc6 3. Ne7 + 4. Nxc6**
RESULT:	White wins a knight (1–0).
ATTACK PROFILE:	Instead of moving his knight to safety, Black protected it. A temporary sacrifice on c6 leads to a knight fork at e7, regaining the rook and putting White a piece ahead.
OBSERVATION:	Move it, and you might not have to defend it.

POSITION: W: Kg1 Qb3 Bb1 Nd5 Pf2 Pg3 (5)
B: Kc8 Qd7 Rd8 Pb7 Pc7 Pg7 (6)

WHITE
TO MOVE

ENEMY MOVE:	1. . . . 0-0-0
PRIMARY TARGET:	d7
SECONDARY TARGETS:	c8/f5
BATTLE TACTIC:	Fork
RESPONSE:	2. Bf5 3. Ne7+ 4. Nxf5
RESULT:	White wins the queen for a bishop (1–0).
ATTACK PROFILE:	Black defended his queenside by castling. Suddenly, king and queen are on the same diagonal. Using a pin, White's bishop attracts the queen to a forkable square, and a knight fork wins.
OBSERVATION:	A bishop often shills for a knight.

POSITION: W: Kc1 Qf3 Rd1 Nc3 Pb2 Pc2 Pe4 (7)
B: Kg8 Qg6 Rb8 Bd7 Pe5 Pf7 Pg7 (7)

BLACK
TO MOVE

ENEMY MOVE:	1. 0-0-0
PRIMARY TARGET:	f3
SECONDARY TARGET:	d1
BATTLE TACTIC:	Skewer
RESPONSE:	1. . . . Bg4 2. . . . Bxd1
RESULT:	Black wins the exchange (0–1).
ATTACK PROFILE:	Though White's rook is active, castling queenside has also placed it in line with the queen. Black capitalizes by a bishop skewer at g4. The queen moves, the rook is devoured.
OBSERVATION:	Even castling can be risky.

POSITION: W: Kc1 Qe4 Rd1 Rd2 Pa2 Pb2 Pc2 (7)
B: Kg8 Qh6 Rd8 Rf8 Pb6 Pg7 (6)

BLACK
TO MOVE

ENEMY MOVE:	1. 0-0-0
PRIMARY TARGET:	c1
SECONDARY TARGET:	None
BATTLE TACTIC:	Mating net
RESPONSE:	1. . . . Qxd2 + 2. . . . Rf1 + 3. . . . Rxd1 + +
RESULT:	White is mated (0–1).
ATTACK PROFILE:	White castled to protect d2, but this fails to an explosive queen sacrifice. After the queen is taken, Black's f8-rook checks on White's weakened front rank, and mate results when either Black rook captures on d1.
OBSERVATION:	A weak back rank can break your back.

POSITION: W: Ke1 Bc4 Nc3 Ne5 Pb2 Pf2 (6)
B: Ke8 Qd8 Bd1 Bf8 Pd6 Ph5 (6)

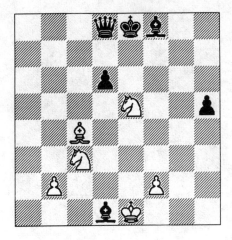

WHITE
TO MOVE

ENEMY MOVE:	1. . . . Bg4xd1
PRIMARY TARGET:	e8
SECONDARY TARGET:	None
BATTLE TACTIC:	Mating net
RESPONSE:	2. Bf7 + 3. Nd5 + +
RESULT:	Black is mated (1–0).
ATTACK PROFILE:	Black has a bishop on d1 because of his greedy capture of White's queen, made without careful analysis. Consequently, Black is mated in two moves by a team of three minor pieces.
OBSERVATION:	King for queen is not a good trade.

POSITION: W: Ke1 Bd2 Nc3 Pb2 Pe4 Pf2 (6)
B: Kg8 Bb4 Nf6 Pc6 Pf7 Pg7 (6)

BLACK
TO MOVE

ENEMY MOVE:	**1. Bc1-d2**
PRIMARY TARGET:	c3
SECONDARY TARGET:	e4
BATTLE TACTIC:	Removing the guard
RESPONSE:	**1. . . . Bxc3 2. . . . Nxe4**
RESULT:	Black wins a pawn (0–1).
ATTACK PROFILE:	White broke the pin on his knight with his bishop, restoring the knight's defense of e4. The knight, however, is captured by Black's bishop. After White takes back on c3, Black's knight is free to collar the e-pawn.
OBSERVATION:	Unpinning a piece doesn't stop its removal.

POSITION: W: Ke1 Qd2 Ra1 Pa3 Pb2 Pe2 (6)
B: Ke8 Qa5 Nb4 Pb5 Pc4 Pg5 (6)

BLACK
TO MOVE

ENEMY MOVE:	**1. Qd1-d2**
PRIMARY TARGET:	c2
SECONDARY TARGET:	a1
BATTLE TACTIC:	Fork
RESPONSE:	**1. . . . Nc2+ 2. . . . Qxd2+ 3. . . . Nxa1**
RESULT:	Black wins the rook (0–1).
ATTACK PROFILE:	White's queen pinned the knight to prevent a discovery, but on d2 the queen is vulnerable to a stratagem. By checking on c2, Black uncovers a pin of his own. Unable to capture the knight, White loses the rook after Black trades queens.
OBSERVATION:	May the better pin win.

POSITION: W: Ke1 Qd1 Bc1 Nd2 Pb3 Pf2 (6)
B: Ke8 Qd8 Ba6 Nd5 Pe4 Pg6 (6)

BLACK
TO MOVE

ENEMY MOVE:	1. Nb1-d2
PRIMARY TARGET:	d1
SECONDARY TARGET:	e1
BATTLE TACTIC:	Trapping
RESPONSE:	1. . . . Ne3 2. . . . Qh4 + +
RESULT:	Black wins the queen or mates (0–1).
ATTACK PROFILE:	By developing his knight to the second rank, White clogged his position and weakened e3. Black's knight exploits this by invading on the weakened square. To save the queen, White must take the knight, but that allows a queen mate at h4.
OBSERVATION:	Close ranks and there's nowhere to go.

POSITION: W: Kg1 Qd3 Rf1 Bc1 Pf2 Pg2 (6)
B: Kg8 Qa5 Rf8 Bc8 Pb6 Pf7 Pg7 (7)

BLACK
TO MOVE

ENEMY MOVE:	**1. Qc2xd3**
PRIMARY TARGET:	d3
SECONDARY TARGET:	f1
BATTLE TACTIC:	Skewer
RESPONSE:	**1. . . . Ba6 2. . . . Bxf1**
RESULT:	Black wins the exchange (0–1).
ATTACK PROFILE:	White's queen is on an undesirable diagonal: the one occupied by his rook. Black's bishop goes to a6, skewering the two major pieces. The queen moves, and the rook is captured. White gets the bishop, but it's not enough.
OBSERVATION:	In a skewer, the second piece is the first to fall.

POSITION: W: Ke1 Qd1 Nf3 Pd2 Pf2 Pg2 (6)
B: Kg8 Qd8 Bd3 Pa6 Pd6 Pg7 (6)

WHITE
TO MOVE

ENEMY MOVE:	1. . . . Bf5-d3
PRIMARY TARGET:	g8
SECONDARY TARGET:	d3
BATTLE TACTIC:	Fork
RESPONSE:	2. Qb3 + 3. Qxd3
RESULT:	White wins the bishop (1–0).
ATTACK PROFILE:	Black positioned his bishop to harass the White King, but the bishop itself is unsupported and assailable. So is Black's king, and White takes advantage of the disarray by a queen check at b3, gaining the bishop.
OBSERVATION:	Be careful in the enemy camp. It's dangerous there.

POSITION: W: Ke1 Bd3 Nf3 Pc2 Pf2 Pg2 (6)
B: Kf8 Bf5 Ne7 Pb7 Pd6 Pe5 (6)

BLACK
TO MOVE

ENEMY MOVE:	**1. Be2-d3**
PRIMARY TARGETS:	d3/f3
SECONDARY TARGET:	None
BATTLE TACTIC:	Fork
RESPONSE:	**1. . . . e4**
RESULT:	Black wins a piece for a pawn (0–1).
ATTACK PROFILE:	White tried to guard his c-pawn with the bishop, but that walks into a lunging e-pawn. The pawn fork insures the gain of either White's bishop or knight, with White getting only a pawn in the transaction.
OBSERVATION:	When confronting an advanced pawn, beware of a fork.

POSITION: W: Kg1 Qd4 Nf3 Pc4 Pg2 (5)
B: Kg8 Qc7 Be7 Pf7 Pg7 (5)

BLACK
TO MOVE

ENEMY MOVE:	**1. Qd1xd4**
PRIMARY TARGET:	d4
SECONDARY TARGET:	g1
BATTLE TACTIC:	Pin
RESPONSE:	**1. . . . Bc5**
RESULT:	Black wins the queen for a bishop (0–1).
ATTACK PROFILE:	If White is castled kingside, and the a7-g1 diagonal is open, it's unwise for White's queen to occupy d4. Black's dark-square bishop could pin the queen to the king.
OBSERVATION:	Occupying a line doesn't necessarily strengthen the line.

POSITION: W: Ke1 Qd1 Nd4 Pb2 Pe4 Pf2 (6)
B: Kg8 Qd8 Nb4 Pb7 Pf7 Pg7 (6)

BLACK
TO MOVE

ENEMY MOVE:	1. Nf3xd4
PRIMARY TARGET:	d4
SECONDARY TARGET:	e1
BATTLE TACTIC:	Fork
RESPONSE:	1. . . . Qxd4 2. . . . Nc2 + 3. . . . Nxd4
RESULT:	Black wins a knight (0–1).
ATTACK PROFILE:	The squares d4 and e1 are a knight's jump from c2. Black's queen takes the d4-knight. If White's queen takes back, c2 is left unguarded and Black's knight forks there. Otherwise, Black simply steals White's knight.
OBSERVATION:	Some forks happen, others are set up.

POSITION: W: Kg1 Qd1 Bd3 Pb2 Pf2 (5)
B: Ke8 Qd4 Be7 Pa6 Pf7 (5)

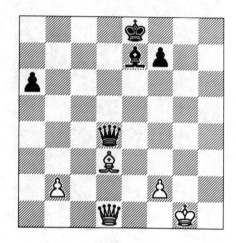

WHITE
TO MOVE

ENEMY MOVE:	**1. . . . Qd8xd4**
PRIMARY TARGET:	e8
SECONDARY TARGET:	d4
BATTLE TACTIC:	Discovery
RESPONSE:	**2. Bb5 + 3. Qxd4**
RESULT:	White wins the queen for a bishop (1–0).
ATTACK PROFILE:	White starts with a bishop check at b5. True, the bishop can be captured by the a-pawn, but the check ties Black's hands, preventing him from saving his queen. White experiences no repercussions in taking it.
OBSERVATION:	No queen is invincible.

85

W: Kg1 Qd5 Nf3 Pb3 Pf2 Pg2 (6)
B: Kg8 Qd8 Bd6 Pc7 Pf7 Pg7 (6)

BLACK
TO MOVE

ENEMY MOVE:	**1. Qd1xd5**
PRIMARY TARGET:	g1
SECONDARY TARGET:	d5
BATTLE TACTIC:	Discovery
RESPONSE:	**1 . . . Bh2 + 2. . . . Qxd5**
RESULT:	Black wins the queen for a bishop (0–1).
ATTACK PROFILE:	Black's bishop separates the two queens on the d-file. By checking on h2, Black loses the bishop but freezes the action so that White can't move his queen, which is then vaporized.
OBSERVATION:	There's no recovery from check by discovery.

POSITION: W: Kg1 Nd5 Pb2 Pc2 Pf3 Pg2 (6)
B: Kb7 Bd6 Pb4 Pc7 Pf4 Pg7 (6)

BLACK
TO MOVE

ENEMY MOVE:	**1. Nc3-d5**
PRIMARY TARGET:	d5
SECONDARY TARGET:	None
BATTLE TACTIC:	Trapping
RESPONSE:	**1. . . . c6**
RESULT:	Black wins the knight for a pawn (0–1).
ATTACK PROFILE:	White's knight went to d5 to escape the attack of Black's b-pawn. Normally, centralization is a good policy, but here it results in loss of the knight. Black simply attacks it with the c-pawn.
OBSERVATION:	If the center is tenuous, a knight may be untenable.

POSITION: W: Ke1 Bb5 Nc4 Pb2 Pf2 Pg2 (6)
B: Ke8 Bc8 Nc6 Pb7 Pd5 Pe5 (6)

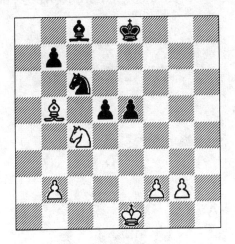

WHITE
TO MOVE

ENEMY MOVE:	**1. . . . d6-d5**
PRIMARY TARGET:	e5
SECONDARY TARGET:	c6
BATTLE TACTIC:	Pin
RESPONSE:	**2. Nxe5**
RESULT:	White wins a pawn (1–0).
ATTACK PROFILE:	The advance of the d-pawn has unhinged the e-pawn. Since Black's knight is pinned, White's knight takes the e-pawn for free. After Black's bishop goes to d7 to guard c6, White eliminates all minor pieces and wins the pawn ending.
OBSERVATION:	Pawn moves can spawn countermoves.

105

POSITION: W: Kg1 Qd1 Bb3 Nf3 Pa2 Pe4 Pf2 Pg2 (8)

B: Ke8 Qd8 Bc8 Ne7 Pb5 Pd6 Pe5 Pf7 (8)

WHITE
TO MOVE

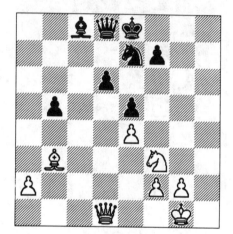

ENEMY MOVE:	1. . . . d7-d6
PRIMARY TARGET:	e5
SECONDARY TARGETS:	f7/d8
BATTLE TACTIC:	Pin
RESPONSE:	2. Nxe5 3. Bxf7+ 4. Qxd8
RESULT:	White wins at least a pawn (1–0).
ATTACK PROFILE:	Black's e-pawn is guarded, but it's not safe from capture! White's knight takes it. If the d-pawn takes back, opening the center, White's bishop captures on f7, deflecting Black's king from the defense of his queen. White's queen would then do a number on Black's.
OBSERVATION:	If a position can be ripped open, it can be ripped off.

POSITION: W: Kg2 Rf1 Pa4 Pe4 Pf3 Ph2 (6)
B: Ke8 Bd6 Nf6 Pc7 Pg7 (5)

WHITE
TO MOVE

ENEMY MOVE:	**1. . . . Bf8-d6**
PRIMARY TARGET:	e5
SECONDARY TARGET:	e8
BATTLE TACTIC:	Pin
RESPONSE:	**2. e5 3. Re1 4. f4**
RESULT:	White wins a minor piece for a pawn (1–0).
ATTACK PROFILE:	The bishop went to d6 to prevent the advance of the e-pawn. White pushes it anyway! After the bishop takes, the rook pins bishop to king. If the knight defends from d7, White piles on by moving the f-pawn. The bishop is lost.
OBSERVATION:	An uncastled king is vulnerable in an open center.

POSITION: W: Kb1 Bd3 Ne2 Pd4 Pe4 Pf3 Pg3 (7)
B: Kg8 Bd6 Nf6 Pc7 Pe5 Pf7 (6)

**WHITE
TO MOVE**

ENEMY MOVE:	1. . . . Be7-d6
PRIMARY TARGET:	e5
SECONDARY TARGETS:	d6/f6
BATTLE TACTIC:	Fork
RESPONSE:	2. dxe5 3. f4 4. e5
RESULT:	White wins a minor piece for a pawn (1–0).
ATTACK PROFILE:	Black defended his e-pawn instead of exchanging it for White's d-pawn. So White captures on e5. After Black recaptures, White's f-pawn advances one square, the bishop withdraws to d6, and White has a pawn fork on e5, gaining a minor piece.
OBSERVATION:	Sometimes you have to trade it to avoid losing it.

91

POSITION: W: Kg1 Qe2 Nf5 Pc3 Pf2 Pg2 (6)
B: Kg8 Qd7 Nc6 Pc5 Pf7 Pg7 (6)

WHITE
TO MOVE

ENEMY MOVE:	1. . . . Qd8-d7
PRIMARY TARGET:	g7
SECONDARY TARGET:	d7
BATTLE TACTIC:	Double threat
RESPONSE:	2. Qg4 3. Nh6+ 4. Qxd7
RESULT:	White wins the queen (1–0).
ATTACK PROFILE:	Black's queen attacks the f5-knight, so White's queen defends it from g4, threatening mate at g7. Black can stop the mate by moving either the f-pawn or the g-pawn one square, but then a knight check at h6 uncovers an attack by White's queen against Black's. Black's queen goes down.
OBSERVATION:	Don't walk into discoveries. Run away from them.

POSITION: W: Kg1 Qa4 Be2 Nf3 Pc4 Pf2 Pg2 (7)
          B: Ke8 Qd7 Bh5 Nc7 Pe5 Pf6 (6)

WHITE
TO MOVE

ENEMY MOVE:	**1. . . . Qd8-d7**
PRIMARY TARGET:	d7
SECONDARY TARGETS:	e5/h5
BATTLE TACTIC:	Discovery
RESPONSE:	**2. Qxd7+ 3. Nxe5+ 4. Bxh5**
RESULT:	White wins a pawn (1–0).
ATTACK PROFILE:	White trades queens on d7. After Black takes back with the king, White's knight takes the e5-pawn. This attack also unleashes a discovery to the h5-bishop. The knight is captured, but White retaliates by gobbling Black's bishop.
OBSERVATION:	Try two at once and one might succeed.

93

POSITITON: W: Kg1 Qd1 Bb5 Nc3 Pb2 Pf2 Pg2 (7)
B: Ke8 Qd8 Bd7 Ng4 Pb7 Pe7 Pf7 (7)

WHITE
TO MOVE

ENEMY MOVE:	1. . . . Bc8-d7
PRIMARY TARGET:	g4
SECONDARY TARGET:	None
BATTLE TACTIC:	Pin
RESPONSE:	2. Qxg4
RESULT:	White wins a knight (1–0).
ATTACK PROFILE:	Black's bishop blocks the check and seems to defend the knight on g4. But since the bishop is pinned along the a4-e8 diagonal, it's unable to capture on g4 should the knight be taken. Thus, the queen filches it.
OBSERVATION:	Pinned appearances can be deceiving.

POSITION: W: Kg2 Qd2 Bh6 Nc3 Pb2 Pf2 Pg3 (7)
B: Kg8 Qa5 Rd8 Bh8 Pb7 Pd6 Pf7 Pg6 Ph7 (9)

WHITE
TO MOVE

ENEMY MOVE:	1. . . . Rf8-d8
PRIMARY TARGET:	g8
SECONDARY TARGET:	a5
BATTLE TACTIC:	Discovery
RESPONSE:	2. Nd5 3. Qxa5
RESULT:	White wins the queen (1–0).
ATTACK PROFILE:	Black's rook occupies d8, preventing the queen from retreating there if necessary (to guard e7, for example). White's knight leaps to d5, threatening mate at e7 and uncovering an attack on Black's queen for White's. Black must stop the mate, abandoning his queen to its fate.
OBSERVATION:	Give yourself no way out and you're out.

POSITION: W: Kf1 Rc1 Nd5 Pb2 Pf2 Ph6 (6)
B: Kg8 Qd8 Pb7 Pf7 Ph7 (5)

WHITE
TO MOVE

ENEMY MOVE:	1. . . . Qe7-d8
PRIMARY TARGET:	d8
SECONDARY TARGETS:	g8/c8
BATTLE TACTIC:	Fork
RESPONSE:	2. Rc8 3. Ne7 + 4. Nxc8
RESULT:	White wins the queen for a rook (1–0).
ATTACK PROFILE:	Black's queen prevents a back-rank mate, but a clever rook sacrifice forces it to a forkable square (c8). After the knight checks on e7, the queen is consumed.
OBSERVATION:	Though individually weaker, a team of two can beat one.

POSITION: W: Kh1 Qd8 Rd1 Pa2 Pg2 Ph2 (6)
B: Kh8 Qe8 Re2 Pb6 Pg7 Ph6 (6)

BLACK
TO MOVE

ENEMY MOVE:	**1. Qd5-d8**
PRIMARY TARGET:	h1
SECONDARY TARGET:	d8
BATTLE TACTIC:	Removing the guard
RESPONSE:	**1. . . . Re1 + 2. . . . Qxd8**
RESULT:	Black wins the queen for a rook (0–1).
ATTACK PROFILE:	If Black takes the queen, the d1-rook captures on d8 with check, preventing Black's rook from mating on e1. But if Black checks on e1 first, White's rook must take Black's, leaving White's queen hanging on d8.
OBSERVATION:	Having coverage against mate doesn't mean you're insured.

POSITION: W: Ka2 Ne1 Pg3 Ph2 (4)
B: Kc3 Bg6 Pf6 Pg4 (4)

BLACK
TO MOVE

ENEMY MOVE:	**1. Nf3-e1**
PRIMARY TARGET:	e1
SECONDARY TARGET:	None
BATTLE TACTIC:	Trapping
RESPONSE:	**1. . . . Be4 2. . . Kd2 3. . . . Kxe1**
RESULT:	Black wins the knight (0–1).
ATTACK PROFILE:	The knight, streaking in the wrong direction, blundered onto the front rank. The bishop denies it its last escape square, and the king adds the knight to his collection.
OBSERVATION:	The edge is seldom the right place for a knight.

POSITION: W: Kg1 Qd1 Re1 Pb3 Pf2 Pg3 (6)
B: Kg8 Qa5 Bh3 Ne5 Pc6 Pf7 Pg7 (7)

BLACK
TO MOVE

ENEMY MOVE:	**1. Rf1-e1**
PRIMARY TARGET:	e1
SECONDARY TARGETS:	g1/f3
BATTLE TACTIC:	Fork
RESPONSE:	**1. . . . Qxe1 + 2. . . . Nf3 + 3. . . . Nxe1**
RESULT:	Black wins the rook (0–1).
ATTACK PROFILE:	White's queen is guarding e1 and f3. Black's queen obliterates the rook, forcing White's queen out of position. The knight exploits this, regaining the queen after the check on f3.
OBSERVATION:	Not even a queen can be everywhere at once.

99

POSITION: W: Ke1 Ra1 Bd2 Na3 Pb2 Pg2 (6)
         B: Kg8 Rf8 Bc5 Nd4 Pb7 Pe4 Pg7 (7)

BLACK
TO MOVE

ENEMY MOVE:	**1. Kf1-e1**
PRIMARY TARGET:	a3
SECONDARY TARGETS:	e1/a1
BATTLE TACTIC:	Fork
RESPONSE:	**1. . . . Bxa3 2. . . . Nc2 3. . . . Nxa1**
RESULT:	Black wins at least the exchange (0–1).
ATTACK PROFILE:	The a3-knight, guarding c2, holds down the fort. But Black exchanges bishop for knight, enabling Black's own knight to occupy c2 with check. The rook is then confiscated.
OBSERVATION:	If it thwarts your attack, get rid of it.

100

POSITION: W: Ke1 Qd1 Bf1 Nd2 Ne2 Pf2 (6)
B: Ke8 Qd8 Bc5 Bg4 Nf6 Pc6 Pg7 (7)

BLACK
TO MOVE

ENEMY MOVE:	**1. Ng1-e2**
PRIMARY TARGET:	f2
SECONDARY TARGET:	e1
BATTLE TACTIC:	Mating attack
RESPONSE:	**1. . . . Qb6 2. . . . Bxf2 +**
RESULT:	Black wins a pawn (0–1).
ATTACK PROFILE:	White's troops are so congested that he's defenseless against the battery of bishop and queen along the a7-g1 diagonal. Only an outside force could bolster f2.
OBSERVATION:	Maintain equilibrium. If your opponent congests, you should ingest.

101

POSITION: W: Kg2 Rf1 Nf3 Pa3 Pf2 (5)
B: Ke8 Ra8 Be2 Pa7 Pf7 (5)

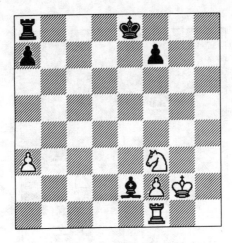

WHITE
TO MOVE

ENEMY MOVE:	**1. . . . Ba6xe2**
PRIMARY TARGET:	e2
SECONDARY TARGET:	e8
BATTLE TACTIC:	Pin
RESPONSE:	**2. Re1 3. Rxe2**
RESULT:	White wins the bishop (1–0).
ATTACK PROFILE:	It looks good for Black, for he's forking rook and knight. But White can play his rook to e1, pinning bishop to king. Suddenly, it looks bad.
OBSERVATION:	Whoever castles first owns the e-file.

POSITION: W: Kg1 Qe2 Rf1 Bg2 Nf3 Pc2 Pf2 (7)
B: Kg8 Qf6 Rd8 Bg4 Nc6 Pf7 Pg7 (7)

**BLACK
TO MOVE**

ENEMY MOVE:	**1. Qd1-e2**
PRIMARY TARGET:	e2
SECONDARY TARGET:	f3
BATTLE TACTIC:	Pin
RESPONSE:	**1. . . . Nd4 2. . . . Nxf3 +**
RESULT:	Black wins at least a knight (0–1).
ATTACK PROFILE:	White's queen got off the d-file and maintains its protection of the f3-knight. But since the f3-knight is pinned, Black's knight enters at d4 with devastating effect. White saves his queen but loses the knight without a fight.
OBSERVATION:	You can expedite losing by getting pinned.

103

BLACK
TO MOVE

ENEMY MOVE:	**1. Bc1-e3**
PRIMARY TARGET:	c4
SECONDARY TARGETS:	c3/e3
BATTLE TACTIC:	Fork
RESPONSE:	**1. . . . d5 2. . . . d4**
RESULT:	Black wins a piece for a pawn (0–1).
ATTACK PROFILE:	White's pieces are positioned around the middle, but Black has the only center pawn. He advances it, attacking the c4-bishop. If the bishop moves to safety, the d-pawn advances again, forking knight and e3-bishop.
OBSERVATION:	Being in the center has a downside. You're easier to attack.

POSITION: W: Ke1 Bf1 Nd2 Pe3 Pf2 (5)
B: Ke8 Bg4 Nd4 Pc7 (4)

BLACK
TO MOVE

ENEMY MOVE:	**1. e2-e3**
PRIMARY TARGET:	e1
SECONDARY TARGET:	None
BATTLE TACTIC:	Mating net
RESPONSE:	**1. . . . Nc2 + +**
RESULT:	White is mated on the move (0–1).
ATTACK PROFILE:	White pushed the e-pawn to drive away the knight, but this automatic attack opened the d1-g4 diagonal, leaving White's king without a safe move. The knight check at c2 is fatal.
OBSERVATION:	To see the counter to a blind attack, just play it.

POSITION: W: Ke1 Qe3 Nc3 Pb2 Pc2 (5)
B: Ka7 Re8 Be7 Nf6 Pa6 Pg7 (6)

BLACK
TO MOVE

ENEMY MOVE:	**1. Qd2-e3 +**
PRIMARY TARGET:	e3
SECONDARY TARGET:	e1
BATTLE TACTIC:	Pin
RESPONSE:	**1. . . . Bc5 2. . . . Nxe8**
RESULT:	Black wins the queen for a rook (0–1).
ATTACK PROFILE:	White's queen gave a pointless check, which is answered by a winning pin. The best that White can do is to surrender queen for rook.
OBSERVATION:	Only novices have the right to give lots of pointless checks.

POSITION: W: Kg1 Rf1 Bb3 Pa2 Pf2 Pg2 (6)
B: Ke8 Ra8 Ne4 Pa7 Pd6 Pe5 (6)

WHITE
TO MOVE

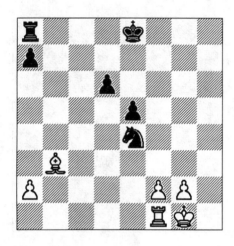

ENEMY MOVE:	1. . . . Nf6xe4
PRIMARY TARGET:	a8
SECONDARY TARGET:	e4
BATTLE TACTIC:	Fork
RESPONSE:	2. Bd5
RESULT:	White wins the knight (1–0).
ATTACK PROFILE:	Black's knight and rook occupy the same diagonal because he neglected development and took a pawn. He should have moved the rook. Now the bishop wins one of these two hapless soldiers by going to d5.
OBSERVATION:	Get them out or your opponent will take them out.

POSITION: W: Kc1 Qd2 Rd1 Pb2 Pc2 Pf2 (6)
B: Ke8 Qe4 Rd8 Pa7 Pd6 Pf7 (6)

WHITE
TO MOVE

ENEMY MOVE:	1. . . . Qe7xe4
PRIMARY TARGET:	e4
SECONDARY TARGET:	e8
BATTLE TACTIC:	Pin
RESPONSE:	**2. Re1**
RESULT:	White wins the queen for a rook (1–0).
ATTACK PROFILE:	Black's queen and king are lined up on the e-file. White's rook, being an appropriate straight-line piece, occupies e1 and pins the queen. It's that simple.
OBSERVATION:	The queen is too valuable to lose for a mere pawn.

POSITION: W: Kg1 Qd2 Ne4 Pf2 Pg2 Ph2 (6)
B: Kg8 Qd8 Bd6 Pe6 Pf7 Pg7 Ph6 (7)

BLACK
TO MOVE

ENEMY MOVE:	**1. Nc3-e4**
PRIMARY TARGET:	h2
SECONDARY TARGET:	e4
BATTLE TACTIC:	Fork
RESPONSE:	**1. . . . Bxh2+ 2. . . . Qh4+ 3. . . . Qxe4**
RESULT:	Black wins a pawn (0–1).
ATTACK PROFILE:	White's knight assails the bishop, but is unprotected on e4. Black cashes in by sacrificing the bishop on h2. After the king captures the bishop, Black's queen forks on h4, regaining the sacrificed piece.
OBSERVATION:	Throw punches, but don't let your guard down.

POSITION: W: Kc1 Qe2 Be3 Pc2 Pe4 Pg2 (6)
B: Ke8 Qd8 Be5 Pb4 Pf7 Pg6 (6)

WHITE
TO MOVE

ENEMY MOVE:	**1. . . . Bg7xe5**
PRIMARY TARGET:	e8
SECONDARY TARGET:	e5
BATTLE TACTIC:	Fork
RESPONSE:	**2. Qb5 + 3. Qxe5**
RESULT:	White wins a bishop (1–0).
ATTACK PROFILE:	Material is even, but Black is terribly exposed. A queen fork at b5 attacks king and bishop. The bishop has seen better days.
OBSERVATION:	Don't begin operations with an exposed king.

POSITION: W: Kg1 Qf2 Be3 Pc2 Pg3 Ph3 (6)
B: Ke8 Qe5 Rh8 Pc6 Pf7 Ph5 (6)

WHITE
TO MOVE

ENEMY MOVE:	**1. . . . Qc7xe5**
PRIMARY TARGET:	e5
SECONDARY TARGET:	h8
BATTLE TACTIC:	Skewer
RESPONSE:	**2. Bd4 3. Bxh8**
RESULT:	White wins a rook (1–0).
ATTACK PROFILE:	Black's queen is aggressively placed in the center, but it's also on the a1-h8 diagonal, as is Black's rook. From d4, White's bishop has a diagonal day, appropriating the cornered rook.
OBSERVATION:	You can't stay up the exchange if you lose your rook.

POSITION: W: Ke1 Qd1 Bc4 Ne5 Pd4 Pe3 Ph2 (7)
B: Kg8 Qd8 Bc8 Nd7 Pa7 Pf7 Pg6 (7)

BLACK
TO MOVE

ENEMY MOVE:	**1. Nf3-e5**
PRIMARY TARGET:	e5
SECONDARY TARGETS:	e1/c4
BATTLE TACTIC:	Fork
RESPONSE:	**1. . . . Nxe5 2. . . . Qh4 + 3. . . . Qxc4**
RESULT:	Black wins a bishop (0–1).
ATTACK PROFILE:	White is pressing the attack against f7, but Black's defense is an easy one. First, he trades off one of the aggressors, the knight at e5. Then a queen check at h4 wins the c4-bishop. Black also wins if he reverses his first and second moves.
OBSERVATION:	If it doesn't matter, start with a capture.

POSITION: W: Kg2 Bb5 Na4 Pe4 Pf4 Ph3 (6)
B: Kg8 Be6 Nd7 Pb6 Pe5 Pf6 (6)

WHITE
TO MOVE

ENEMY MOVE:	**1. . . . Bg4-e6**
PRIMARY TARGET:	e6
SECONDARY TARGET:	d7
BATTLE TACTIC:	Removing the guard
RESPONSE:	**2. f5**
RESULT:	White wins a piece for a pawn (1–0).
ATTACK PROFILE:	Black's bishop guards his knight, so White advances to drive it away. If the bishop moves to safety, it abandons the d7-knight to White's bishop. If it stays put, the f-pawn puts it back in the box.
OBSERVATION:	Don't place your pieces where they must be defended.

113

POSITION: W: Kg2 Qd5 Be2 Bg5 Pc4 Pe4 (6)
B: Ke8 Qb8 Bf8 Nd7 Pd6 Pe6 Pf7 (7)

WHITE
TO MOVE

ENEMY MOVE:	1. . . . e7-e6
PRIMARY TARGET:	e8
SECONDARY TARGET:	None
BATTLE TACTIC:	Mating net
RESPONSE:	2. Qxe6 + 3. Bh5 + +
RESULT:	Black is mated (1–0).
ATTACK PROFILE:	Black tries to snipe at the queen, but moving the e-pawn leaves his king without a safe place to go. By sacrificing the big one on e6, White lures the f-pawn out of position, and a bishop check at h5 is mate.
OBSERVATION:	Stick out your pawn and it can be snipped off.

114

POSITION: W: Kg1 Qd2 Nc3 Ne6 Pb2 Pg2 (6)

B: Ke8 Qd8 Bg7 Ne7 Pd5 Pg6 (6)

BLACK
TO MOVE

ENEMY MOVE:	**1. Nd4-e6**
PRIMARY TARGET:	g1
SECONDARY TARGET:	e6
BATTLE TACTIC:	Fork
RESPONSE:	**1. . . . Qb6+ 2. . . . Qxe6**
RESULT:	Black wins a knight (0–1).
ATTACK PROFILE:	White's knight invades, forking Black's queen and bishop. But Black has a queen check on b6, rebuffing the incursion. White gets out of check and the knight is reduced to nothing.
OBSERVATION:	For your sake, never attack for attack's sake.

115

W: Kg1 Qd1 Bd5 Nf3 Pc2 Pe3 Pg2 (7)
W: Ke8 Qc7 Bg4 Ne7 Pc5 Pf7 (6)

WHITE
TO MOVE

ENEMY MOVE:	1. . . . Ng8-e7
PRIMARY TARGET:	f7
SECONDARY TARGET:	g4
BATTLE TACTIC:	Discovery
RESPONSE:	2. Bxf7 + 3. Ng5 + 4. Qxg4
RESULT:	White wins a pawn (1–0).
ATTACK PROFILE:	Uncertain where to go, Black developed his knight to e7. A better square is f6, to guard the g4-bishop. After the error, White sacrifices the bishop on f7 and follows with a knight check at g5. This uncovers a queen attack to the g4-bishop, which is undefended and lost.
OBSERVATION:	If you're not sure what to do, don't do it.

POSITION: W: Kg1 Re1 Bg5 Nc3 Pe4 Pf2 Pg2 (7)
B: Ke8 Rb6 Be7 Nf6 Pd6 Pe5 (6)

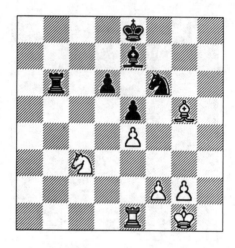

WHITE
TO MOVE

ENEMY MOVE:	**1. . . . Bf8-e7**
PRIMARY TARGET:	f6
SECONDARY TARGET:	b6
BATTLE TACTIC:	Fork
RESPONSE:	**2. Bxf6 3. Nd5 4. Nxb6**
RESULT:	White wins the exchange (1–0).
ATTACK PROFILE:	The focus is d5. Black's knight, standing sentinel, is captured. After recapture on f6, White's knight invades the d5-outpost. Black retreats the bishop to d8 to minimize his loss. (Instead of a full piece, he loses rook for knight.)
OBSERVATION:	To usurp a square, eliminate its defenders.

POSITION: W: Kh1 Rd1 Ne7 Pc4 Pe4 Ph4 (6)
B: Kg8 Qd2 Rd8 Bg7 Pb7 Pd6 Pf7 (7)

BLACK
TO MOVE

ENEMY MOVE:	1. Nd5xe7 +
PRIMARY TARGET:	d1
SECONDARY TARGET:	e7
BATTLE TACTIC:	Double threat
RESPONSE:	1. . . . Kf8 2. . . . Kxe7
RESULT:	Black wins the knight (0–1).
ATTACK PROFILE:	Instead of capturing Black's queen, White interposed the capture of a pawn on e7, figuring it was safe because it was with check. Black's king gets out of check by attacking the knight. Since White must capture the queen, he loses the knight without a fight.
OBSERVATION:	Switch plans, but don't imperil your pieces.

POSITION: W: Kg1 Rf1 Ba4 Nf3 Pc3 Pd4 Pe4 Pg2
(8)

B: Kg8 Re8 Bc8 Nc6 Pb7 Pd6 Pe5 Pf7
(8)

WHITE
TO MOVE

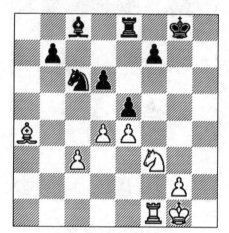

ENEMY MOVE:	1. . . . Rf8-e8
PRIMARY TARGET:	c6
SECONDARY TARGET:	e8
BATTLE TACTIC:	Pin
RESPONSE:	2. d5 3. dxc6
RESULT:	White wins a knight for a pawn (1–0).
ATTACK PROFILE:	If it were Black's move, he would exchange pawns on d4 and win the e-pawn. But it's White's turn, and the advance of the d-pawn closes the center and wins the hapless knight, pinned to the rook at e8 by the a4-bishop.
OBSERVATION:	Your attack means nothing if your opponent's comes first.

119

POSITION: W: Kc1 Rd1 Bh4 Pb5 Pc4 Pe4 Pf3 (7)
B: Kg8 Rf8 Be8 Pb7 Pf7 Pg7 (6)

WHITE
TO MOVE

ENEMY MOVE:	**1. . . . Bc6-e8**
PRIMARY TARGET:	f8
SECONDARY TARGET:	None
BATTLE TACTIC:	Trapping
RESPONSE:	**2. Be7 3. Bxf8**
RESULT:	White wins the exchange (1–0).
ATTACK PROFILE:	Black is down a pawn, though with bishops of opposite colors, he ordinarily might have chances to draw. But here, White's bishop simply attacks the rook and wins the exchange.
OBSERVATION:	Exchange, but don't lose the exchange.

POSITION: W: Kg1 Qd1 Re1 Bb3 Pa2 Pd4 Pg2 (7)
B: Kg8 Qb8 Re8 Bf8 Pf7 Ph7 (6)

WHITE
TO MOVE

ENEMY MOVE:	**1. . . . Rd8-e8**
PRIMARY TARGET:	f7
SECONDARY TARGET:	e8
BATTLE TACTIC:	Skewer
RESPONSE:	**2. Bxf7+ 3. Qh5+ 4. Qxe8**
RESULT:	White wins a rook and a pawn for a bishop (1–0).
ATTACK PROFILE:	Black's rook challenges the e-file, offering a trade, but White has a winning sacrifice on f7. After the king takes back, a queen check on h5 skewers king and rook, winning the rook.
OBSERVATION:	When you're behind, trades usually help your opponent.

121

POSITION: W: Kf1 Ra1 Bc1 Pa4 Pf2 Ph2 (6)
B: Kg8 Re8 Bc8 Pa5 Pf7 Pg7 (6)

BLACK
TO MOVE

ENEMY MOVE:	**1. Ke1-f1**
PRIMARY TARGET:	f1
SECONDARY TARGET:	None
BATTLE TACTIC:	Mating net
RESPONSE:	**1. . . . Bh3 + 2. . . . Re1 + +**
RESULT:	Black forces mate (0–1).
ATTACK PROFILE:	White pays for moving his king into a box. Black checks at h3, seizing control of g2 and driving the king away from e1. The rook then mates along the back rank.
OBSERVATION:	Play dead and they bury you.

POSITION: W: Kg1 Qg5 Ra7 Bf1 Pf2 Pg3 Ph2 (7)
B: Kg8 Qh3 Re8 Bd7 Pf7 Pg7 Ph7 (7)

BLACK
TO MOVE

ENEMY MOVE:	**1. Be2-f1**
PRIMARY TARGET:	g1
SECONDARY TARGET:	None
BATTLE TACTIC:	Mating net
RESPONSE:	**1. . . . Qxf1+ 2. . . . Bh3+ 3. . . . Re1++**
RESULT:	Black forces mate (0–1).
ATTACK PROFILE:	Black's bishop guards the queen, and White's bishop attacks it. So Black forces mate by sacrificing queen for bishop. After White takes back with the king, Black's bishop checks on h3 and the rook follows with mate at e1.
OBSERVATION:	What's a bishop between combatants?

123

POSITION: W: Kg1 Qb3 Rf1 Nc4 Pf2 Pf3 Ph2 (7)
B: Kg8 Qh3 Re8 Bd4 Pf7 Pg6 (6)

BLACK
TO MOVE

ENEMY MOVE:	**1. Ra1-f1**
PRIMARY TARGET:	g1
SECONDARY TARGET:	None
BATTLE TACTIC:	Mating net
RESPONSE:	**1. . . . Bxf2+**
RESULT:	Black forces mate (0–1).
ATTACK PROFILE:	The bishop captures on f2. If the rook takes the bishop, Black's rook checks on e1 and mates next. Or if the king takes the bishop, Black's queen captures on h2, also mating. And if the bishop isn't taken at all, Black's queen takes the rook next move, giving mate to the cornered king.
OBSERVATION:	If the first take fails, do a second take.

POSITION: W: Kh1 Qb1 Rd1 Ng3 Pd5 Pg2 Ph3 (7)
B: Kh8 Qf2 Rf8 Ne5 Pd6 Pg7 Ph7 (7)

WHITE
TO MOVE

ENEMY MOVE:	1. . . . Qf6xf2
PRIMARY TARGET:	f2
SECONDARY TARGET:	f8
BATTLE TACTIC:	Skewer
RESPONSE:	2. Rf1
RESULT:	White wins the queen for a rook (1–0).
ATTACK PROFILE:	The queen on f2 attacks the g3-knight. But the knight supports the shift of White's rook to f1, skewering queen and rook. If the queen moves off the f-file, White's rook mates by capturing on f8. Black gets only a rook for the queen.
OBSERVATION:	Don't get caught between shifts.

125

W: Kg1 Rf1 Rf2 Pd3 Pg2 (5)
B: Kg8 Rf8 Bf6 Pb5 Pg4 (5)

BLACK
TO MOVE

ENEMY MOVE:	**1. Rb2-f2**
PRIMARY TARGET:	f2
SECONDARY TARGET:	g1
BATTLE TACTIC:	Pin
RESPONSE:	**1. . . . Bd4 2. . . . b4 3. . . . Rxf2**
RESULT:	Black wins the pawn ending (0–1).
ATTACK PROFILE:	First Black's bishop pins the rook at f2. White moves the g-pawn, Black the b-pawn. Next move, Black swaps all four pieces on f2. With nothing left to stop the b-pawn, White can merely watch Black make a new queen.
OBSERVATION:	For starters, eliminate the stoppers.

143

POSITION: W: Kg1 Qf2 Rf1 Bc4 Pg3 Ph2 (6)
B: Kh7 Qh3 Bb7 Bf6 Pg6 (5)

BLACK
TO MOVE

ENEMY MOVE:	1. Qe3-f2
PRIMARY TARGET:	g1
SECONDARY TARGET:	None
BATTLE TACTIC:	Mating net
RESPONSE:	1. . . . Bd4 2. . . . Qg2 + +
RESULT:	Black forces mate (0–1).
ATTACK PROFILE:	White's queen threatens the bishop on f6 and guards against mate at g2. It can't do both, however, and Black proves this by pinning the queen, moving the bishop from f6 to d4. The queen can defend itself by taking the bishop, but it can't protect g2 to prevent mate.
OBSERVATION:	Get pinned, and you're no good to anyone.

127

POSITION: W: Ke1 Qd1 Be2 Pd5 Pf3 Pg2 Ph3 (7)
B: Kg8 Qf6 Ne4 Pd4 Pf7 Pg7 (6)

BLACK
TO MOVE

ENEMY MOVE:	1. f2-f3
PRIMARY TARGET:	e1
SECONDARY TARGET:	None
BATTLE TACTIC:	Mating net
RESPONSE:	1. . . . Qh4+ 2. . . . Qxg3+ 3. . . . Qf2++
RESULT:	Black forces mate (0–1).
ATTACK PROFILE:	White pushed the f-pawn to kick out the knight, but that opened the e1-h4 diagonal for Black's queen. The queen checks at h4, captures the g-pawn attempting a futile block, and concludes on f2 with the fool's mate.
OBSERVATION:	The road to losing is paved with bad pawn moves.

POSITION: W: Kg1 Qf3 Bc4 Pc3 Pe4 Pg2 Ph2 (7)
B: Ke8 Qc8 Nc6 Pa6 Pb7 Pd6 Pf7 Pg6 (8)

BLACK
TO MOVE

ENEMY MOVE:	**1. Qe2-f3**	
PRIMARY TARGET:	f3	
SECONDARY TARGET:	c4	
BATTLE TACTIC:	Fork	
RESPONSE:	**1. . . . Ne5**	
RESULT:	Black wins the bishop for a pawn (0 – 1).	
ATTACK PROFILE:	White prepares a "scholar's check" at f7—queen supported by bishop—but this is an empty threat. A straightforward knight's move defends f7 and doubly attacks c4 and f3. White obtains a pawn for the bishop, no more.	
OBSERVATION:	Aspire to ideal threats, but play real ones.	

129

BLACK
TO MOVE

ENEMY MOVE:	**1. Ra3-f3**
PRIMARY TARGET:	f3
SECONDARY TARGETS:	e2/f1
BATTLE TACTIC:	Skewer
RESPONSE:	**1. . . . Nd4 2. . . . Nxe2+ 3. . . . Bb5**
RESULT:	Black wins the exchange (0–1).
ATTACK PROFILE:	White's rooks threaten the f-pawn. Black's knight reacts by invading d4, forcing the rook to reposition to e3 or f2. The knight then takes on e2, the rook takes back, and Black's bishop swings to b5. The skewer insures that White loses a rook for the bishop.
OBSERVATION:	Don't double rooks on diagonals.

POSITION: W: Kf1 Ra1 Bf4 Nd4 Pb2 Pe4 Pf5 Ph2 (8)

B: Kb8 Rf7 Bc8 Bg7 Pb7 Pe6 Pe7 Ph4 (8)

BLACK
TO MOVE

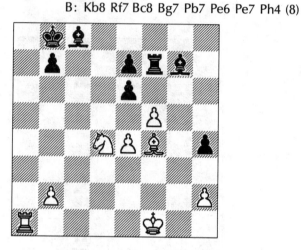

ENEMY MOVE:	**1. Be3-f4 +**
PRIMARY TARGETS:	d4/f4
SECONDARY TARGET:	None
BATTLE TACTIC:	Fork
RESPONSE:	**1. . . . e5**
RESULT:	Black wins a piece for a pawn (0–1).
ATTACK PROFILE:	White's bishop check would be great if it weren't for one ugly fact: the e-pawn can advance, ending the check and forking the bishop and knight. White can only decide which loss is least painful.
OBSERVATION:	See check, give check—a familiar losing formula.

131

POSITION: W: Kc3 Ne3 Pd3 Pe4 Pg2 (5)
B: Ke7 Rf4 Pe5 Pg5 (4)

WHITE
TO MOVE

ENEMY MOVE:	**1. . . . Rg4-f4**
PRIMARY TARGET:	e7
SECONDARY TARGET:	f4
BATTLE TACTIC:	Fork
RESPONSE:	**2. Nd5 + 3. Nxf4**
RESULT:	White wins the exchange (1–0).
ATTACK PROFILE:	Black is ahead by a rook for a knight, but he's down a pawn. By checking on d5, and then capturing on f4, the knight garners back the exchange and leaves White with a winning endgame.
OBSERVATION:	No rook is safe when a knight springs.

POSITION: W: Kc1 Qf4 Nd3 Pb2 Pc2 Pg2 (6)
B: Kg8 Qb5 Bf6 Pb7 Pd6 Pg7 (6)

BLACK
TO MOVE

ENEMY MOVE:	**1. Qd2xf4**
PRIMARY TARGET:	f4
SECONDARY TARGET:	c1
BATTLE TACTIC:	Pin
RESPONSE:	**1. . . . Bg5**
RESULT:	Black wins the queen for a bishop (0–1).
ATTACK PROFILE:	White's catch was the f-pawn, which he riskily took with his queen. But he overlooked a bishop move to g5, pinning queen to king.
OBSERVATION:	Catch, but don't get caught.

POSITION: W: Kg2 Qf5 Rh1 Ng1 Pd4 Pg3 Ph3 (7)
B: Kg7 Qd6 Rf8 Nf6 Pd5 Pg5 Ph5 (7)

BLACK
TO MOVE

ENEMY MOVE:	**1. Qd3xf5**
PRIMARY TARGET:	f5
SECONDARY TARGET:	f2
BATTLE TACTIC:	Pin
RESPONSE:	**1. . . . Ne4**
RESULT:	Black wins queen for rook (0–1).
ATTACK PROFILE:	Black's knight goes to e4, uncovering an attack by the rook against the queen. If White's queen checks on e5, Black's queen captures it for free, since White is unable to take back because of mate hanging at f2. To minimize the loss, the queen should be surrendered for the rook.
OBSERVATION:	If you can't trap it, leave it without choice.

POSITION: W: Kg2 Qd3 Ne4 Pb2 Pf2 Pg3 (6)
B: Kg8 Qe7 Ra8 Pf5 Pg7 Ph7 (6)

WHITE
TO MOVE

ENEMY MOVE:	1. . . . f7-f5
PRIMARY TARGET:	g8
SECONDARY TARGET:	a8
BATTLE TACTIC:	Fork
RESPONSE:	2. Qd5 + 3. Qxa8 +
RESULT:	White wins a rook (1–0).
ATTACK PROFILE:	Black got aggressive and charged the knight. But White sidesteps the assault with a queen check at d5, which also lines up the rook. Next move, the rook is extinguished, along with Black's hopes.
OBSERVATION:	Look to both sides of the board, with both sides of the brain.

135

POSITION: W: Kg1 Qc2 Nd2 Pb2 Pe4 Pg2 (6)
B: Kg8 Qg7 Bb7 Pc7 Pe5 Pf5 (6)

WHITE
TO MOVE

ENEMY MOVE:	1. . . . f7-f5
PRIMARY TARGET:	g8
SECONDARY TARGET:	b7
BATTLE TACTIC:	Fork
RESPONSE:	2. Qb3 + 3. Qxb7
RESULT:	White wins the bishop (1–0).
ATTACK PROFILE:	Black has fantastic plans, hoping White will capture on f5 and allow mate on g2. Yet the f5-pawn's advance is Janus-faced. It fuels the attack, but also exposes Black's king to check from b3. The queen fork wins the bishop.
OBSERVATION:	Fantasizing is not planning.

POSITION: W: Kb2 Re1 Bb3 Ne5 (4)
           B: Kh8 Rf8 Nd6 Pf6 Pg7 Ph7 (6)

WHITE
TO MOVE

ENEMY MOVE:	1. . . . f7-f6
PRIMARY TARGET:	h8
SECONDARY TARGET:	None
BATTLE TACTIC:	Mating net
RESPONSE:	2. Ng6 + 3. Rh1 + +
RESULT:	White forces mate (1–0).
ATTACK PROFILE:	Black's f-pawn, under siege by White's bishop and knight, moved out of attack, threatening the knight. But this advance laid bare the a2-g8 line while also weakening g6. The winning variant: a knight sacrifice on g6, exploding open the h-file. The rook mates at h1.
OBSERVATION:	Every analysis has a silver line.

137

POSITION: W: Kg1 Qd1 Ne5 Pd4 Pg2 (5)
B: Ke8 Qd8 Bd6 Pd5 Pf6 (5)

WHITE
TO MOVE

ENEMY MOVE:	1. . . . f7-f6
PRIMARY TARGET:	e8
SECONDARY TARGET:	None
BATTLE TACTIC:	Mating net
RESPONSE:	2. Qh5 + 3. Qf7 + +
RESULT:	White forces mate (1–0).
ATTACK PROFILE:	Trying to drive away the knight with the f-pawn only makes Black's king vulnerable to a queen check at h5. The king moves and the queen mates at f7, protected by the knight, the piece Black wanted to make disappear.
OBSERVATION:	Threaten, but don't ignore the threat.

POSITION: W: Kg2 Qd2 Bc2 Be3 Pd4 Pf2 Pg3 Ph4 (8)

B: Kg8 Qf6 Bf8 Ne7 Pe6 Pf7 Pg7 Ph6 (8)

WHITE
TO MOVE

ENEMY MOVE:	**1. . . . Qf5-f6**
PRIMARY TARGET:	f6
SECONDARY TARGET:	None
BATTLE TACTIC:	Trapping
RESPONSE:	**2. Bg5 3. hxg5**
RESULT:	White wins the queen for two pieces (1–0).
ATTACK PROFILE:	Black's queen backed into a trap at f6, encircled and shackled by its own units. White's bishop issues the first salvo on g5, and the h-pawn follows with the second. On its knees, the queen moves to f5 or g6, and White must expend another bishop to capture it.
OBSERVATION:	Surround yourself with friendly forces and there may be nowhere to go.

139

POSITION: W: Kc1 Bf7 Pb2 Pf2 Ph2 (5)
B: Kd7 Nf6 Pc6 Pe7 Ph7 (5)

BLACK
TO MOVE

ENEMY MOVE:	**1. Ba2xf7**
PRIMARY TARGET:	f7
SECONDARY TARGET:	None
BATTLE TACTIC:	Trapping
RESPONSE:	**1. . . . e6 2. . . . Ke7**
RESULT:	Black wins a bishop for a pawn (0–1).
ATTACK PROFILE:	The bishop captured on f7, but when the black pawn moves to e6 there's no escape. Since every square the bishop could go to is guarded, the king expunges it.
OBSERVATION:	For a bishop, a short reach means a short life.

POSITION: W: Kc1 Bb3 Nf7 Pc2 Pf2 (5)
B: Kg8 Nd4 Pa7 Pd6 Ph7 (5)

BLACK
TO MOVE

ENEMY MOVE:	**1. Ne5xf7**
PRIMARY TARGET:	b3
SECONDARY TARGET:	f7
BATTLE TACTIC:	Removing the guard
RESPONSE:	**1. . . . Nxb3 + 2. . . . Kxf7**
RESULT:	Black wins a piece (0–1).
ATTACK PROFILE:	White's knight, threatening two pawns, is protected by the bishop. Black removes the bishop with check. Afterward, White's unprotected knight is eradicated. Black's pawns have a secure future.
OBSERVATION:	Knock out the base and the building topples.

POSITION: W: Kc1 Bc4 Rf7 Pb3 Pd4 Pg5 (6)
B: Kg8 Rc8 Bb7 Pa7 Pg6 Ph7 (6)

BLACK
TO MOVE

ENEMY MOVE:	**1. Rf1xf7**
PRIMARY TARGET:	c4
SECONDARY TARGET:	f7
BATTLE TACTIC:	Removing the guard
RESPONSE:	**1. . . . Rxc4 + 2. . . . Kxf7**
RESULT:	Black wins a bishop (0–1).
ATTACK PROFILE:	White's bishop protects the rook, which seems to be threatening a murderous discovered check. But forget discoveries, since the supporting bishop is pinned and capturable. Black takes it with check, and then collects the rook.
OBSERVATION:	When the protectors are pinned, the position can go to pieces.

POSITION: W: Kg1 Re8 Bc1 Pf2 Pg2 (5)
B: Kg8 Ra2 Bf8 Pf7 Pg6 Ph7 (6)

**WHITE
TO MOVE**

ENEMY MOVE:	**1. . . . Bg7-f8**
PRIMARY TARGET:	f8
SECONDARY TARGET:	None
BATTLE TACTIC:	Mating net
RESPONSE:	**2. Bh6**
RESULT:	White forces mate (1–0).
ATTACK PROFILE:	If given a chance to play his next move, Black could unpin his king or use his rook to pin White's bishop. But it's White's move, and the bishop goes to h6, avoiding being pinned and insuring mate at f8.
OBSERVATION:	The loser is often too late.

143

POSITION: W: Kh1 Qg1 Ra1 Bc1 Pa5 Pg2 Ph3 (7)
B: Kg8 Qe7 Rf8 Ba6 Pg7 (5)

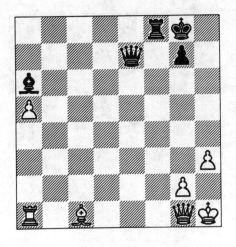

WHITE
TO MOVE

ENEMY MOVE:	**1. . . . Ra8-f8**
PRIMARY TARGET:	e7
SECONDARY TARGET:	f8
BATTLE TACTIC:	Skewer
RESPONSE:	**2. Ba3 3. Bxf8**
RESULT:	White wins the exchange (1–0).
ATTACK PROFILE:	Black has a threat: to pin White's queen along the first rank. White counters by developing the bishop to a3, defending his home rank with the rook, and skewering queen and rook.
OBSERVATION:	Simple threats: It's remarkable how often they're missed.

POSITION: W: Kh2 Qg4 Be3 Pd4 Pe5 Pg2 Ph3 (7)
B: Kg8 Qd8 Rf8 Pf7 Pg7 (5)

WHITE
TO MOVE

ENEMY MOVE:	**1. . . . 0-0**
PRIMARY TARGET:	g7
SECONDARY TARGET:	f8
BATTLE TACTIC:	Pin
RESPONSE:	**2. Bh6 3. Bxf8**
RESULT:	White wins the exchange (1–0).
ATTACK PROFILE:	Black castled to guard the g-pawn. White attacks it anyway from h6 with the bishop, which can't be taken because of the pin. To stop the mate, Black advances the g-pawn one square, deserting the rook for the bishop.
OBSERVATION:	Castle, but not into trouble.

145

POSITION: W: Kh1 Ra2 Rg1 Bc2 Ph2 (5)
B: Kb8 Re8 Rg8 Bh3 Pb7 (5)

BLACK
TO MOVE

ENEMY MOVE:	**1. Rf1-g1**
PRIMARY TARGET:	h1
SECONDARY TARGET:	None
BATTLE TACTIC:	Mating net
RESPONSE:	**1. . . . Bg2 + 2. . . . Re1 + 3. . . . Rxg1 + +**
RESULT:	Black forces mate (0–1).
ATTACK PROFILE:	The g1-rook is burdened with too many tasks, guarding g2 and the back rank. A bishop check forces the rook off the back row, enabling the e8-rook to intrude with check. The g2-rook must block the check, and either black rook captures with mate.
OBSERVATION:	It's hard to hold down two jobs.

POSITION: W: Kg1 Qb4 Rb1 Pg2 Ph2 (5)
B: Kh8 Qf6 Rf8 Pg7 Ph7 (5)

**BLACK
TO MOVE**

ENEMY MOVE:	**1. Kh1-g1**
PRIMARY TARGET:	g1
SECONDARY TARGET:	None
BATTLE TACTIC:	Mating net
RESPONSE:	**1. . . . Qf2+ 2. . . . Qf1+ 3. . . . Rxf1++**
RESULT:	Black forces mate (0–1).
ATTACK PROFILE:	White has just played the king to g1 to stave off a back-rank invasion. But with Black's queen and rook doubled on the f-file, a queen check on f2 drives the king back into the corner. Mate ensues on f1, according to Black's original plan.
OBSERVATION:	Two against one, the king comes undone.

POSITION: W: Kg1 Qd2 Rf1 Be3 Pd4 Pg2 (6)
          B: Kg8 Qd8 Re8 Bb6 Pf7 Pg7 (6)

BLACK
TO MOVE

ENEMY MOVE:	**1. 0-0**
PRIMARY TARGET:	e3
SECONDARY TARGET:	d4/g1
BATTLE TACTIC:	Pin
RESPONSE:	**1. . . . Rxe3**
RESULT:	Black wins at least a bishop (0–1).
ATTACK PROFILE:	White castled to get out of the pin along the e-file, only to step into a new pinning alignment. Black simply takes White's bishop. If the queen recaptures, Black's bishop captures on d4, winning the queen.
OBSERVATION:	Sometimes even the safest-looking moves can fail.

148

POSITION: W: Ke1 Qd1 Rh1 Nf3 Pe4 Pf2 (6)
B: Kf7 Qg2 Ra8 Nf6 Pe5 Ph7 (6)

WHITE
TO MOVE

ENEMY MOVE:	**1. . . . Qg5xg2**
PRIMARY TARGET:	g2
SECONDARY TARGETS:	f7/h3
BATTLE TACTIC:	Fork
RESPONSE:	**2. Rg1**
RESULT:	White wins the queen for a rook (1–0).
ATTACK PROFILE:	Black's queen has penetrated deep into White's territory, attacking the h1-rook. White saves the rook and strikes at the queen. Its only good square is h3, but White's knight can fork h3 and f7 from g5. Black might as well give up the queen for the rook.
OBSERVATION:	If it's lost, get something for it.

149

POSITION: W: Kh1 Qe3 Rg2 Nc3 Pf2 Ph2 (6)
B: Kc8 Qh5 Rg6 Nf3 Pb5 Pc7 (6)

BLACK
TO MOVE

ENEMY MOVE:	**1. Rg1-g2**
PRIMARY TARGET:	h1
SECONDARY TARGET:	None
BATTLE TACTIC:	Mating net
RESPONSE:	1. . . . Qxh2 + 2. . . . Rg1 + +
RESULT:	Black forces mate (0–1).
ATTACK PROFILE:	White's rook appears to hold the fort. Black dispels the illusion by sacrificing the queen on h2. The rook must take the queen, and Black's rook, supported by the knight, mates on g1.
OBSERVATION:	Don't get rooked.

POSITION: W: Kg2 Qd1 Be3 Bf1 Pf2 Ph2 (6)
B: Ke8 Qg5 Bg4 Pc6 Ph5 (5)

BLACK
TO MOVE

ENEMY MOVE:	**1. Kh1xg2**
PRIMARY TARGET:	g2
SECONDARY TARGET:	None
BATTLE TACTIC:	Mating net
RESPONSE:	**1. . . . Bf3 + 2. . . . Qg4 + +**
RESULT:	Black forces mate (0–1).
ATTACK PROFILE:	White fearlessly exposed his king, counting on his extra piece and an attack on Black's queen. But the double check freezes the action, and whether White's king takes the bishop or moves to h3, the queen still mates on g4.
OBSERVATION:	Better to be a coward and live.

POSITION: W: Kg1 Qd1 Nc3 Pb2 Pf2 Pg3 (6)
B: Kg7 Qh4 Bb6 Pb7 Pf7 Pg6 (6)

BLACK
TO MOVE

ENEMY MOVE:	1. g2-g3
PRIMARY TARGET:	g3
SECONDARY TARGET:	f2
BATTLE TACTIC:	Pin
RESPONSE:	1. . . . Qxg3 +
RESULT:	Black wins two pawns (0–1).
ATTACK PROFILE:	White attacks the queen, which can defend itself admirably by taking the pawn on g3. Her highness can't be captured because of the bishop's pin on the f-pawn, which also plummets.
OBSERVATION:	Pinned protection is pathetic.

POSITION: W: Ke1 Qg3 Pc3 Pf2 Pg2 Ph3 (6)
B: Ke8 Bb6 Ne5 Nf6 Pc6 Pe6 Pf7 Pg7 (8)

BLACK
TO MOVE

ENEMY MOVE:	**1. Qf3-g3**
PRIMARY TARGET:	f2
SECONDARY TARGETS:	e1/g3
BATTLE TACTIC:	Fork
RESPONSE:	**1. . . . Bxf2 +**
RESULT:	Black wins the queen for two pieces (0–1).
ATTACK PROFILE:	White's queen attacks e5 and g7 while guarding the hole on d3. But the three pieces humiliate the queen, beginning with a bishop sacrifice on f2. If the king takes, the f6-knight forks on e4. If the queen takes, the e5-knight forks on d3.
OBSERVATION:	The whole is greater than the hole.

POSITION: W: Kg1 Bg3 Nc3 Pb2 Pf2 Pg2 Ph2 (7)
B: Kg8 Bd6 Nf6 Pc7 Pf5 Pg5 Ph6 (7)

BLACK
TO MOVE

ENEMY MOVE:	1. Bh4-g3
PRIMARY TARGET:	f4
SECONDARY TARGET:	None
BATTLE TACTIC:	Trapping
RESPONSE:	1. . . . f4
RESULT:	Black wins the bishop for a pawn (0–1).
ATTACK PROFILE:	White seeks an exchange of bishops, but Black frustrates this by advancing the f-pawn. White's bishop goes down ingloriously.
OBSERVATION:	Rampaging pawns can romp.

POSITION: W: Ke1 Bd4 Bf3 Pb4 Pg4 (5)
B: Ke7 Bc8 Nf6 Pd6 Pe6 Pf7 (6)

BLACK
TO MOVE

ENEMY MOVE:	**1. g2-g4**
PRIMARY TARGET:	d4
SECONDARY TARGET:	g4
BATTLE TACTIC:	Double threat
RESPONSE:	**1. . . . e5**
RESULT:	Black wins a pawn (0–1).
ATTACK PROFILE:	White pushed the g-pawn, and Black counters with the e-pawn, making two threats. If White retreats the d4-bishop, Black captures on g4. If instead White counterattacks with the g-pawn, Black takes the d4-bishop, White captures the knight, and Black's king takes back on f6. White loses a pawn.
OBSERVATION:	Push the pawn with the most bite.

155

POSITION: W: Ke1 Qd1 Bd3 Nc3 Pb2 Pe5 (6)
B: Ke8 Qd8 Bc8 Ng4 Pe7 Pf7 (6)

WHITE
TO MOVE

ENEMY MOVE:	1. . . . Nf6-g4
PRIMARY TARGET:	e8
SECONDARY TARGET:	g4
BATTLE TACTIC:	Pin
RESPONSE:	2. Bb5 + 3. Qxg4
RESULT:	White wins the knight (1–0).
ATTACK PROFILE:	Black's knight on g4 is guarded by the bishop. White's bishop check changes that. Black must block with his bishop or lose the queen. But once on d7 and pinned, the bishop cannot respond to a capture on g4. White's queen takes the knight without hassle.
OBSERVATION:	You don't have to start in a pin to wind up in one.

POSITION: W: Ke1 Qd1 Bb3 Bc1 Nf3 Pc3 Pf2 (7)
B: Ke8 Qd8 Bf8 Bg4 Ne5 Pd6 Pf7 (7)

WHITE
TO MOVE

ENEMY MOVE:	1. . . . Bc8-g4
PRIMARY TARGET:	e5
SECONDARY TARGET:	g4
BATTLE TACTIC:	Pin
RESPONSE:	2. Nxe5
RESULT:	White wins at least a piece (1–0).
ATTACK PROFILE:	Black's g4-bishop pins the knight. White, however, has an unpinning combination, beginning by taking Black's knight. If the g4-bishop takes the queen, White mates after the b3-bishop captures on f7 and the c1-bishop checks on g5. Otherwise, White steals Black's knight.
OBSERVATION:	Pinning is good, mating is better.

157

W: Ke1 Qf3 Bg5 Pd4 Pe3 Pf2 (6)
B: Ke8 Qd8 Nf6 Pb7 Pc6 Pf7 (6)

BLACK
TO MOVE

ENEMY MOVE:	1. Bf4-g5
PRIMARY TARGET:	e1
SECONDARY TARGET:	g5
BATTLE TACTIC:	Fork
RESPONSE:	1. . . . Qa5 + 2. . . . Qxg5
RESULT:	Black wins the bishop (0–1).
ATTACK PROFILE:	On the surface, White's pinning bishop sortie seems to win the knight. But Black, with the move, unpins by a queen check, which also attacks the bishop. The bishop, obstructed by its own e3-pawn, can't block the check and is claimed by the queen.
OBSERVATION:	The pin is mighty, but so is the fork.

POSITION: W: Ke1 Rd1 Bg5 Ng1 Pe4 Pf2 (6)
B: Ke8 Rg8 Bc5 Nf6 Pe5 Pf7 Pg7 (7)

BLACK
TO MOVE

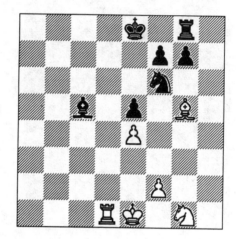

ENEMY MOVE:	1. Bc1-g5
PRIMARY TARGET:	f2
SECONDARY TARGETS:	e4/g5
BATTLE TACTIC:	Fork
RESPONSE:	1. . . . Bxf2+
RESULT:	Black wins a pawn (0–1).
ATTACK PROFILE:	Black's knight can't capture the e-pawn because White's rook mates at d8. But Black has a bishop sacrifice at f2. If the king takes the bishop, the knight captures on e4 with check, winning the g5-bishop. If the king doesn't take back on f2, Black has pilfered a pawn.
OBSERVATION:	If necessary, do it with check.

159

POSITION: W: Kg1 Qd1 Bc1 Pc2 Pe3 Pg2 (6)
B: Kg8 Qg5 Bd5 Pc6 Pf7 Pg7 (6)

WHITE
TO MOVE

ENEMY MOVE:	**1. . . . Qd8-g5**
PRIMARY TARGET:	g5
SECONDARY TARGET:	d5
BATTLE TACTIC:	Discovery
RESPONSE:	**2. e4 3. exd5**
RESULT:	White wins a bishop for a pawn (1–0).
ATTACK PROFILE:	Black's queen and bishop threaten mate at g2. White blocks the bishop's attack by advancing the e-pawn, which also unveils a discovery to Black's queen. The queen must be rescued, so the bishop is relinquished.
OBSERVATION:	A steadfast pawn can save a kingdom.

W: Kg1 Qf5 Bb1 Pc3 Pd4 Pg2 (6)
B: Ke8 Qd8 Bf8 Pd7 Pe7 Pg6 Ph7 (7)

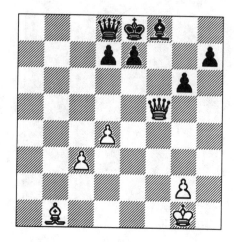

WHITE
TO MOVE

ENEMY MOVE:	1. . . . g7-g6
PRIMARY TARGET:	e8
SECONDARY TARGET:	None
BATTLE TACTIC:	Mating net
RESPONSE:	2. Qxg6 + 3. Bxg6 + +
RESULT:	White forces mate (1–0).
ATTACK PROFILE:	Black tries to scare White's queen, but the shock is Black's after a startling queen sacrifice on g6. The b1-bishop follows through and delivers the coup de grâce.
OBSERVATION:	A blunt weapon also works.

161

POSITION: W: Kb1 Qh5 Rf1 Bb2 Pb3 Pc2 Pg3 (7)
B: Kg8 Qb8 Rc8 Bd6 Pf7 Pg6 Ph7 (7)

WHITE
TO MOVE

ENEMY MOVE:	1. . . . g7-g6
PRIMARY TARGET:	g8
SECONDARY TARGET:	None
BATTLE TACTIC:	Mating net
RESPONSE:	2. Qxh7 + 3. Rh1 + 4. Rh8 + +
RESULT:	White forces mate (1–0).
ATTACK PROFILE:	Black, attacking White's queen, opened the a1-h8 diagonal, which is controlled by the b2-bishop. This fuels White's queen sacrifice on h7, compelling recapture. The rook checks from h1 and, supported by the b2-bishop, mates on h8.
OBSERVATION:	Close one line and you open another.

POSITION: W: Ke1 Qd1 Rh1 Bf3 Pc2 Pf2 Ph2 (7)
B: Ke8 Qg6 Rh8 Bc8 Pb7 Pg7 Ph7 (7)

WHITE
TO MOVE

ENEMY MOVE:	**1. . . . Qg2-g6**
PRIMARY TARGET:	g6
SECONDARY TARGET:	e8
BATTLE TACTIC:	Pin
RESPONSE:	**2. Bh5**
RESULT:	White wins the queen for a bishop (1–0).
ATTACK PROFILE:	Black's queen retreated to the wrong square. The penalty is loss of the queen by the bishop pin at h5. As compensation, Black gets only a bishop.
OBSERVATION:	When you back up, use the rearview mirror.

163

POSITION: W: Kg1 Rf1 Bg7 Pf2 Ph2 (5)
B: Kc8 Rf8 Bb6 Pb7 Pc6 (5)

BLACK
TO MOVE

ENEMY MOVE:	1. Bb2xg7
PRIMARY TARGET:	g7
SECONDARY TARGET:	g1
BATTLE TACTIC:	Pin
RESPONSE:	1. . . . Rg8 2. . . . Rxg7
RESULT:	Black wins a bishop (0–1).
ATTACK PROFILE:	White wanted to win a pawn, so he took one with the bishop. The bishop now attacks the rook, but it's also on the same file as its king. Black saves his rook and pins the audacious unit, cut off from its reinforcements.
OBSERVATION:	Take a good look before taking a bad pawn.

POSITION: W: Ka1 Qb2 Rb1 Pa2 Pf2 (5)
B: Kg8 Qa7 Bg7 Pc7 Pd7 Ph7 (6)

WHITE
TO MOVE

ENEMY MOVE:	**1. . . . Bf8-g7**
PRIMARY TARGET:	g7
SECONDARY TARGET:	g8
BATTLE TACTIC:	Pin
RESPONSE:	**2. Rg1**
RESULT:	White wins at least the bishop (1–0).
ATTACK PROFILE:	White's queen is pinned, and it would be lost if it were not for the fact that the pinning unit itself could be pinned. The rook shifts to g1, freezing the bishop and insuring its demise.
OBSERVATION:	The pin: live by it or die by it.

POSITION: W: Kc1 Rg7 Nc3 Nd4 Pb2 Pg2 (6)
B: Ke8 Rh8 Bc8 Nf6 Pa6 Pf7 Ph6 (7)

BLACK
TO MOVE

ENEMY MOVE:	**1. Rg5xg7**
PRIMARY TARGET:	g7
SECONDARY TARGET:	None
BATTLE TACTIC:	Trapping
RESPONSE:	**1. . . . Nh5**
RESULT:	Black wins a rook for a pawn (0–1).
ATTACK PROFILE:	White's rook conducts a one-unit raid into Black's territory. But when Black's knight attacks it from h5, the rook is without haven. Bye-bye, rook.
OBSERVATION:	As you approach the castle, avoid the moat.

166

POSITION: W: Kc1 Qh6 Ne2 Pc2 Pg6 (5)
B: Kh8 Qc7 Bg8 Pe7 Ph7 (5)

WHITE
TO MOVE

ENEMY MOVE:	1. . . . Be6-g8
PRIMARY TARGET:	h8
SECONDARY TARGET:	None
BATTLE TACTIC:	Mating net
RESPONSE:	2. g7 + +
RESULT:	White mates (1–0).
ATTACK PROFILE:	With Black's last move, he tries to guard h7. But the bishop occupies a possible escape square for the king, and now the pawn advances and mates.
OBSERVATION:	Don't paint your king into the corner.

POSITION: W: Ka1 Qe4 Rg1 Bc2 Pa4 Pd4 (6)
B: Kh8 Qa8 Rf8 Bg8 Pc6 Pd6 Ph7 (7)

WHITE
TO MOVE

ENEMY MOVE:	1. . . . Bf7-g8
PRIMARY TARGET:	h8
SECONDARY TARGET:	None
BATTLE TACTIC:	Mating net
RESPONSE:	2. Rxg8 + 3. Qxh7 + +
RESULT:	White forces mate (1–0).
ATTACK PROFILE:	Black's king and friendly forces are cringing behind a closed door. His h-pawn, though doubly attacked, is defended adequately by the g8-bishop. White's rook holds the key, eliminating the bishop with check. No matter how Black retakes, the queen mates on h7.
OBSERVATION:	Remove the defender, then remove the defended.

168

POSITION: W: Kg1 Rc1 Bg5 Pa3 Pb2 Pg2 (6)
B: Kh8 Rg8 Bc6 Pb7 Ph7 (5)

WHITE
TO MOVE

ENEMY MOVE:	1. . . . Rf8-g8
PRIMARY TARGET:	h8
SECONDARY TARGET:	g7
BATTLE TACTIC:	Pin
RESPONSE:	2. Bf6 +
RESULT:	White wins the exchange (1–0).
ATTACK PROFILE:	Black's rook seems to be pinning the g5-bishop because behind the bishop is an assailable g2-pawn. But White's bishop can unpin with check. Black's rook, the former pinner, must plug up the check, and White gains rook for bishop.
OBSERVATION:	Some pins just don't work.

169

POSITION: W: Kb6 Pa7 (2)
         B: Kf3 Qh1 (2)

WHITE
TO MOVE

ENEMY MOVE:	1. . . . h2-h1(Q)
PRIMARY TARGET:	f3
SECONDARY TARGET:	h1
BATTLE TACTIC:	Skewer
RESPONSE:	2. a8(Q) + 3. Qxh1
RESULT:	White promotes and wins the queen (1–0).
ATTACK PROFILE:	Black has won the race to queen, but now it's White's turn, and he queens with check. Black's king must move out of check, and White's queen acquires its enemy counterpart.
OBSERVATION:	The race is not always to the swiftest.

POSITION: W: Kh1 Qc2 Rc1 Pe4 Pf2 Ph2 (6)
B: Kb8 Qd7 Rg8 Pb7 Pc6 Ph3 (6)

BLACK
TO MOVE

ENEMY MOVE:	**1. Kg1-h1**
PRIMARY TARGET:	h1
SECONDARY TARGET:	None
BATTLE TACTIC:	Mating net
RESPONSE:	**1. . . . Qg4**
RESULT:	Black forces mate (0–1).
ATTACK PROFILE:	White's king bolted in the wrong direction. In the corner, it's trapped and mated after Black's queen bursts in on g4. White can't defend against the two mate threats at f3 and g2.
OBSERVATION:	There's no recess in the corner.

171

POSITION: W: Ke2 Nd2 Pb3 Pc3 Pg3 Ph2 (6)
B: Kb8 Rh1 Pb6 Pg4 (4)

WHITE
TO MOVE

ENEMY MOVE:	**1. . . . Rb1-h1**
PRIMARY TARGET:	h1
SECONDARY TARGET:	None
BATTLE TACTIC:	Trapping
RESPONSE:	**2. Nf1 3. Kf2 4. Kg2**
RESULT:	White wins a rook for a knight (1–0).
ATTACK PROFILE:	The rook tried to ravage, but after the knight repositions to f1, the h-pawn is guarded and the rook encased. The king moves over, forcing the rook to give itself for the knight. White wins the pawn ending without toil.
OBSERVATION:	Rooks start in corners. They don't have to end in them.

POSITION: W: Kg1 Bd4 Nb3 Pf3 Pg2 (5)
B: Kc7 Bh2 Ng4 Pf7 Pg6 (5)

WHITE
TO MOVE

ENEMY MOVE:	**1. . . . Bd6xh2 +**
PRIMARY TARGETS:	g4/h2
SECONDARY TARGET:	None
BATTLE TACTIC:	Double threat
RESPONSE:	**2. Kh1**
RESULT:	White wins a bishop or a knight (1–0).
ATTACK PROFILE:	Although his knight is threatened, Black thought he had time to capture on h2, since it was with check. But White's king steps to the corner, leaving two Black pieces attacked. If the bishop retires to safety, the knight drops. If the knight runs, the bishop flops.
OBSERVATION:	Delay answering a threat, and suddenly you might be facing two threats.

173

POSITION: W: Kg1 Be3 Nc4 Pf3 Pg2 (5)
B: Kc8 Bd6 Nh2 Pc7 Pf7 (5)

WHITE
TO MOVE

ENEMY MOVE:	1. . . . Ng4xh2
PRIMARY TARGET:	d6
SECONDARY TARGET:	h2
BATTLE TACTIC:	Removing the guard
RESPONSE:	2. Nxd6 + 3. Kxh2
RESULT:	White wins a piece (1–0).
ATTACK PROFILE:	It's bad enough that the h2-knight has no escape. It's thinly protected by a distant bishop, and even that support dissolves when the bishop is severed. After the c-pawn recaptures, the black knight vanishes.
OBSERVATION:	Like guardian angels, guardian bishops can suddenly disappear.

POSITION: W: Kf1 Nd3 Pb3 Pf2 Pg5 (5)
B: Ka8 Bh2 Pd4 Pf5 Pg6 (5)

WHITE
TO MOVE

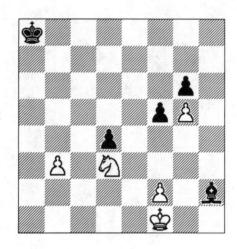

ENEMY MOVE:	**1. . . . Bd6xh2**
PRIMARY TARGET:	h2
SECONDARY TARGET:	None
BATTLE TACTIC:	Trapping
RESPONSE:	**2. f4 3. Kg2 4. Kh3**
RESULT:	White wins a bishop for a pawn (1–0).
ATTACK PROFILE:	The bishop has strayed into enemy territory. By advancing the f-pawn two squares, White reduces the bishop's available space. It can shift to the e1-h4 diagonal, with apparent breathing room, but White's king eventually tracks it down.
OBSERVATION:	Just like that, chessboards can shrink.

175

POSITION: W: Kh1 Qd1 Rf1 Nc3 Pb2 Pg2 Ph3 (7)
B: Kg8 Qh4 Bb6 Ng4 Pa7 Pf7 Ph5 (7)

BLACK
TO MOVE

ENEMY MOVE:	**1. h2-h3**
PRIMARY TARGET:	h1
SECONDARY TARGET:	None
BATTLE TACTIC:	Mating attack
RESPONSE:	**1. . . . Qg3**
RESULT:	Black wins the queen or mates (0–1).
ATTACK PROFILE:	White's kingside is full of holes. Black's queen enters on the weakened g3, menacing mate at h2. If White captures Black's knight with the h-pawn, Black's queen mates by withdrawing to h4. To stop immediate mate, White must surrender his queen for the obstreperous knight.
OBSERVATION:	Avoid Swiss-cheese chess.

POSITION: W: Kh1 Qe1 Bb2 Bg2 Pf2 Ph3 (6)
B: Kh8 Qh5 Bc6 Ng4 Pb7 Pg7 (6)

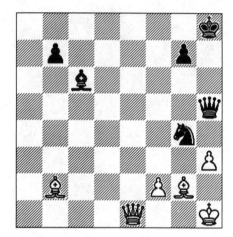

BLACK
TO MOVE

ENEMY MOVE:		**1. h2-h3**
PRIMARY TARGET:		h3
SECONDARY TARGET:		g2
BATTLE TACTIC:		Pin
RESPONSE:		**1. . . . Qxh3 + 2. . . . Qxg2**
RESULT:		Black forces mate (0–1).

ATTACK PROFILE: To stop mate at h2, White had to advance his h-pawn just one square. But the g2-bishop is pinned, and h3 isn't really guarded. Black's queen takes on h3 with check, and mates by capturing the bishop.

OBSERVATION: Healthy pawns are a king's best friends.

POSITION: W: Kg1 Qe2 Rf1 Nf3 Pf2 Pg2 Ph3 (7)
B: Kg8 Qc7 Nc6 Ng4 Pe6 Pf7 (6)

BLACK
TO MOVE

ENEMY MOVE:	**1. h2-h3**
PRIMARY TARGET:	e2
SECONDARY TARGETS:	f3/g1
BATTLE TACTIC:	Double threat
RESPONSE:	**1. . . . Nd4 2. . . . Nxe2 +**
RESULT:	Black wins the queen for a knight (0–1).
ATTACK PROFILE:	Black's knight invades at d4. If White's knight takes on d4, h2 is left unguarded and Black's queen mates. Meanwhile, Black plans to take the overburdened f3-knight and follow with a queen mate at h2. To avert this mate, White captures the g4-knight, abandoning his queen.
OBSERVATION:	Speaking for all defenders, the onus is on us.

POSITION: W: Ke1 Qd1 Bh4 Pc2 Pe2 Pf2 (6)
B: Ke8 Qe7 Nf6 Pb7 Pg7 Ph6 (6)

BLACK
TO MOVE

ENEMY MOVE:	**1. Bg5-h4**
PRIMARY TARGET:	e1
SECONDARY TARGET:	h4
BATTLE TACTIC:	Fork
RESPONSE:	**1. . . . Qb4+ 2. . . . Qxh4**
RESULT:	Black wins the bishop (0 − 1).
ATTACK PROFILE:	White's bishop retreated to h4 to maintain the pin on Black's knight. But at h4 the bishop is vulnerable to a forking queen check on the other side of the board. The queen checks on b4, picking up the bishop horizontally.
OBSERVATION:	Look up and down and across before going back.

179

POSITION: W: Kd2 Nh4 Pg2 Ph2 (4)
B: Kd5 Ne7 Pe4 Pg7 Ph6 (5)

BLACK
TO MOVE

ENEMY MOVE:	**1. Nf3-h4**
PRIMARY TARGET:	h4
SECONDARY TARGET:	None
BATTLE TACTIC:	Trapping
RESPONSE:	**1. . . . g5**
RESULT:	Black wins a knight for a pawn (0–1).
ATTACK PROFILE:	White's knight moved to h4 to escape attack. But where does it go when Black advances the g-pawn two squares? White can get a pawn for the knight, which is some consolation.
OBSERVATION:	It's hard to hide on the side.

180

180

POSITION: W: Ke1 Bh4 Nd2 Pc4 Pf2 (5)
B: Ke7 Bb4 Nf6 Pc5 Pg7 Ph6 (6)

BLACK TO MOVE

ENEMY MOVE:	1. Bg5-h4
PRIMARY TARGET:	h4
SECONDARY TARGET:	d2
BATTLE TACTIC:	Pin
RESPONSE:	1. . . . g5 2. . . . Ne4
RESULT:	Black wins a piece (0–1).
ATTACK PROFILE:	Black wants to pile up on the pinned d2-knight, but his own knight is pinned by White's bishop. So he breaks the pin by advancing the g-pawn two squares. If the bishop retreats to g3, Black's knight invades e4, and the d2-knight is indefensible.
OBSERVATION:	Some pins are more equal than others.

198

181

POSITION: W: Kh1 Qh5 Ba2 Nf1 Pd5 Pg2 Ph2 (7)
B: Kg8 Qe7 Bc8 Ne5 Pb7 Pd6 Pg7 (7)

BLACK
TO MOVE

ENEMY MOVE:	**1. Qd1xh5**
PRIMARY TARGET:	h5
SECONDARY TARGET:	None
BATTLE TACTIC:	Trapping
RESPONSE:	**1. . . . Bg4**
RESULT:	Black wins the queen for a piece (0–1).
ATTACK PROFILE:	White's brash queen is out on a limb, and Black's bishop saws off the branch by moving to g4. The mighty queen falls.
OBSERVATION:	The bigger the piece, the greater the loss when cut down.

POSITION: W: Ke1 Qd1 Nh5 Pc2 Pd3 Pf2 (6)
B: Ke8 Qd8 Nf6 Pe6 Pf7 Pg7 (6)

BLACK
TO MOVE

ENEMY MOVE:	**1. Ng3-h5**
PRIMARY TARGET:	e1
SECONDARY TARGET:	h5
BATTLE TACTIC:	Fork
RESPONSE:	**1. . . . Qa5 + 2. . . . Qxh5**
RESULT:	Black wins a knight (0–1).
ATTACK PROFILE:	White's knight, backed up by the queen, ventured onto the fifth rank. But Black controls his half of the board. The queen goes to a5, forking king and knight. The knight is brutalized.
OBSERVATION:	It can be risky to attack when your king's exposed.

183

POSITION: W: Kc3 Ne3 Pf5 Pg2 (4)
B: Kh7 Bh5 Pf7 (3)

WHITE
TO MOVE

ENEMY MOVE:	**1. . . . Bg6-h5**
PRIMARY TARGET:	h5
SECONDARY TARGET:	None
BATTLE TACTIC:	Trapping
RESPONSE:	**2. g4**
RESULT:	White wins a bishop for a pawn (1–0).
ATTACK PROFILE:	The bishop wants to escape confinement. But White's two-square advance of the g-pawn doesn't permit it, and the bishop suffocates.
OBSERVATION:	It's sad when there's no place to go.

POSITION: W: Kb1 Qh3 Rd1 Bd3 Pb2 Pc3 Pd4 (7)
B: Kg8 Qf8 Re7 Bf6 Pf7 Pg7 Ph6 (6)

WHITE
TO MOVE

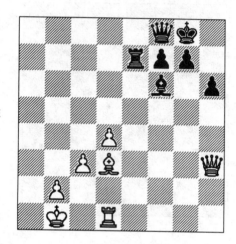

ENEMY MOVE:	**1. . . . h7-h6**
PRIMARY TARGET:	g8
SECONDARY TARGET:	f6
BATTLE TACTIC:	Mating attack
RESPONSE:	**2. Qf5 3. Qxf6**
RESULT:	White wins the bishop (1–0).
ATTACK PROFILE:	Black pushed the wrong pawn to stop mate. He should have moved the g-pawn one square. So White inserts the queen on f5, again threatening mate. Now Black must move the g-pawn anyway, which hangs the f6-bishop. Without ceremony, the queen takes it.
OBSERVATION:	Save the king, and guard/save the bishop.

POSITION: W: Kc1 Qh6 Rh1 Pb2 Pc2 Pg2 Ph5 (7)
B: Kg8 Qc7 Be7 Nf6 Pc4 Pe4 Pf7 Pg6 (8)

BLACK
TO MOVE

ENEMY MOVE:	**1. Qd2xh6**
PRIMARY TARGET:	h6
SECONDARY TARGET:	None
BATTLE TACTIC:	Trapping
RESPONSE:	**1. . . . Nh7 2. . . . Bg5**
RESULT:	Black wins the queen for a piece (0–1).
ATTACK PROFILE:	White's queen frighteningly closes in for the kill. But after the knight retreats to h7, it's White who goes into shock. There's no defense against the bishop move to g5.
OBSERVATION:	Scare tactics fail against good moves.

186

POSITION: W: Ke1 Qd2 Bh6 Ne2 Pc4 Pe4 Pf3 (7)
B: Kg8 Qd8 Bg7 Nf6 Pc7 Pd6 Pf7 Pg6 (8)

BLACK
TO MOVE

ENEMY MOVE:	1. Be3-h6
PRIMARY TARGET:	e4
SECONDARY TARGETS:	e1/h6
BATTLE TACTIC:	Fork
RESPONSE:	1. . . . Nxe4 2. . . . Qh4 +
RESULT:	Black wins a pawn (0–1).
ATTACK PROFILE:	White begins the war with a kingside invasion. Black counters with a knight sacrifice at e4, gaining a pawn and opening the d8-h4 diagonal. After White takes the knight, Black's queen hits the connection point at h4, checking the king and regaining the piece at h6.
OBSERVATION:	The loser confronts, the winner surprises.

POSITION: W: Kg1 Qd3 Bh7 Pc2 Pf2 (5)
B: Kg8 Qd6 Nf4 Pb4 Pd5 Pg7 (6)

BLACK
TO MOVE

ENEMY MOVE:	1. Bf5xh7 +
PRIMARY TARGETS:	d3/h7
SECONDARY TARGET:	f5
BATTLE TACTIC:	Double threat
RESPONSE:	1. . . . Kh8 2. . . . g6
RESULT:	Black wins a bishop for a pawn.
ATTACK PROFILE:	Black's king is attacked, but so are two of White's units. After the king moves to h8, White's queen and bishop remain under fire. Although the queen achieves sanctuary at f5, Black's pawn goes to g6, severing communication. The bishop is trapped and lost.
OBSERVATION:	If you don't give yourself a way out, who will?

188

POSITION: W: Kb1 Bd5 Nh4 Pc2 Pg5 Ph3 (6)
B: Kg8 Bf8 Bh7 Pf7 Pg7 Ph5 (6)

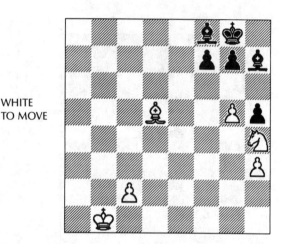

WHITE
TO MOVE

ENEMY MOVE:	**1. . . . Bg6-h7**
PRIMARY TARGET:	h7
SECONDARY TARGET:	None
BATTLE TACTIC:	Trapping
RESPONSE:	**2. g6 3. Nxg6**
RESULT:	White wins a bishop for a pawn (1–0).
ATTACK PROFILE:	Black's forces, huddled together in a tight corner, are stifled by an advancing pawn. If the bishop takes the g-pawn, the knight captures the bishop, and the pinned f-pawn can't take back.
OBSERVATION:	If you're blocked up, you must have had the wrong plan.

189

POSITION: W: Kh1 Qh2 Rb2 Rg1 (4)
B: Kh8 Qd8 Rb8 Rh7 (4)

WHITE
TO MOVE

ENEMY MOVE:	**1. . . . Rb7-h7**
PRIMARY TARGET:	h8
SECONDARY TARGET:	None
BATTLE TACTIC:	Mating net
RESPONSE:	**2. Qxh7 + 3. Rh2 + 4. Rxh4 + +**
RESULT:	White forces mate (1–0).
ATTACK PROFILE:	White's queen is pinned to its king, but White is the boss after sacrificing queen for rook on h7. Black's king recaptures and the b2-rook transfers to h2 with check. Mate can be delayed by blocking at h4 with the queen, but the rook takes and it's still mate.
OBSERVATION:	For linear mate, open the lines.

POSITION: W: Kg1 Qh8 Rf1 Nc3 Pg2 (5)
B: Ka8 Qc8 Bf8 Pa7 Pb7 (5)

BLACK
TO MOVE

ENEMY MOVE:	**1. Qe5xh8**
PRIMARY TARGET:	g1
SECONDARY TARGT:	h8
BATTLE TACTIC:	Discovery
RESPONSE:	**1. . . . Bc5 + 2. . . . Qxh8**
RESULT:	Black wins the queen (0–1).
ATTACK PROFILE:	White is well ahead, having just picked off a rook in the corner. The pendulum shifts to Black when the bishop moves to c5, giving check. This shot unveils a discovered attack on White's queen, which is captured by its opposite number.
OBSERVATION:	Being ahead doesn't guarantee finishing ahead.

POSITION: W: Kh5 Pg6 (2)
B: Kh8 (1)

WHITE
TO MOVE

ENEMY MOVE:	**1. . . . Kg7-h8**
PRIMARY TARGET:	g8
SECONDARY TARGET:	None
BATTLE TACTIC:	Promotion
RESPONSE:	**2. Kh6 3. g7 4. Kh7**
RESULT:	White makes a new queen (1–0).
ATTACK PROFILE:	Black's king should have dropped straight back to g8, for in the corner it gets squeezed out. White wins by advancing: the king to h6, the pawn to g7, the king to h7, and the pawn to g8, making a new queen.
OBSERVATION:	Losing some positions is a matter of technique.

POSITION: W: Kg8 Nh8 (2)
B: Kg6 Ra7 (2)

**BLACK
TO MOVE**

ENEMY MOVE:	**1. h7-h8(N) +**
PRIMARY TARGET:	g8
SECONDARY TARGET:	h8
BATTLE TACTIC:	*Zugzwang*
RESPONSE:	**1. . . . Kf6**
RESULT:	Black wins the knight or mates (0–1).
ATTACK PROFILE:	White's late move was an act of desperation. Black plays the king to f6, creating a *zugzwang*. Any move by White loses. If he moves the king, it's mate. If he moves the knight, it's loss of a piece.
OBSERVATION:	To win, you may have to avoid a last-minute trick.

APPENDICES

(A–G)

A. Review Test

Here is a test of ten problems for review and fun. Fill in the answers, or write them on a separate sheet of paper, and check your results after completing the test. For each example give the TARGETS (group primary and secondary squares together), the BATTLE TACTIC (the name of the main stratagem), and the RESPONSE (the winning side's moves). In each case, the ENEMY MOVE is given to set the stage. Good luck, and happy solving.

193

BLACK TO MOVE

ENEMY MOVE: 1. Nb1-a3

TARGETS:

BATTLE TACTIC:

RESPONSE:

213

194

BLACK TO MOVE

ENEMY MOVE: 1. Bd2xa5

TARGETS:

BATTLE TACTIC:

RESPONSE:

195

WHITE TO MOVE

ENEMY MOVE: 1. . . . b7-b5

TARGETS:

BATTLE TACTIC:

RESPONSE:

196

BLACK TO MOVE

ENEMY MOVE: 1. Rf1-c1

TARGETS:

BATTLE TACTIC:

RESPONSE:

197

WHITE TO MOVE

ENEMY MOVE: 1. . . . Bf8-c5

TARGETS:

BATTLE TACTIC:

RESPONSE:

198

WHITE TO MOVE

ENEMY MOVE: 1. . . . Qb6-c6

TARGETS:

BATTLE TACTIC:

RESPONSE:

199

WHITE TO MOVE

ENEMY MOVE: 1. . . . Nb8-d7

TARGETS:

BATTLE TACTIC:

RESPONSE:

200

WHITE TO MOVE

ENEMY MOVE: 1. . . . Bc8-e6

TARGETS:

BATTLE TACTIC:

RESPONSE:

201

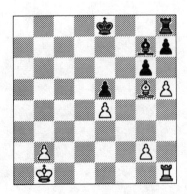

WHITE TO MOVE

ENEMY MOVE: 1. . . . Bf8-g7

TARGETS:

BATTLE TACTIC:

RESPONSE:

202

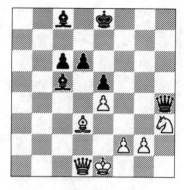

BLACK TO MOVE

ENEMY MOVE: 1. Ng1-h3

TARGETS:

BATTLE TACTIC:

RESPONSE:

B. Review Test Answers

193

TARGETS: a1/a3/d4/g1

BATTLE TACTIC: Fork

RESPONSE: 1. . . . Bxa3 2. . . . Qxd4+ 3. . . . Qxa1

194

TARGETS: a5/e1

BATTLE TACTIC: Fork

RESPONSE: 1. . . . Rxa5 2. . . . Bc3+ 3. . . . Bxa5

195

TARGETS: a8/f7

BATTLE TACTIC: Double threat

RESPONSE: 2. Qd5 3. Qxa8

196

TARGETS: c1/c2/d3

BATTLE TACTIC: Pin

RESPONSE: 1. . . . Bxd3

197

TARGETS: c5/f7

BATTLE TACTIC: Fork

RESPONSE: 2. Bxf7 + 3. Qc4 + 4. Qxc5

198

TARGETS   b5/c6/e8

BATTLE TACTIC: Fork

RESPONSE: 2. Bb5 3. Nc7 + 4. Nxb5

199

TARGETS: f7/g8

BATTLE TACTIC: Skewer

RESPONSE: 2. Nxf7 3. Bd5 + 4. Bxg8

200

TARGETS: e5/e6/e8

BATTLE TACTIC: Fork

RESPONSE: 2. Bxe6 3. Qh5 + 4. Qxe5

201

TARGETS: e5/g7/h8

BATTLE TACTIC: Fork

RESPONSE: 2. h6 3. Bf6 4. Bxe5

202

TARGETS: f2/h3

BATTLE TACTIC: Removing the guard

RESPONSE: 1. . . . Bxh3 2. . . . Qfx 2#

C. Pandolfini's
Short Chess Course

MOVES AND RULES

THE BOARD: An eight-by-eight checkered board of 64 squares, 32 light and 32 dark.

LIGHT SQUARE RULE: Each player must have a light square in their near right corner.

ROWS OF SQUARES: Horizontal rows are ranks, vertical rows are files, and slanted rows of one color are diagonals.

THE PLAYERS: Chess is for two players. The lighter forces are called White, the darker Black.

THE FORCES: Each player starts with 16 units: eight pieces (one king, one queen, two rooks, two bishops, and two knights) and eight pawns. Queens and rooks are major pieces, bishops and knights are minor pieces.

THE OBJECT: To checkmate the enemy king.

THE FIRST MOVE: White goes first, then Black, then White, etc.

A MOVE: The transfer of a unit from one square to another.

A CAPTURE: The removal of a unit from the board by replacing it with a unit belonging to the capturing player.

GENERAL RULES: Move your own units. Capture your opponent's. Move one unit on a turn, except when castling. Move in one direction on a turn, except knights. Units move backward or forward, except pawns. Pawns move only forward. No move is compulsory unless it's the only legal one. The six kinds of units move in different ways. All, except pawns, capture the way they move. Only knights can jump over other units.

THE KING: Moves one square in any direction.

THE ROOK: Moves on ranks or files as many unblocked squares as desired, one direction on a turn.

THE BISHOP: Moves on diagonals of one color as many unblocked squares as desired, one direction on a turn.

THE QUEEN: Moves like a rook or a bishop, but only one direction on a turn.

THE KNIGHT: Moves one square on a rank or file, then two at a right angle, or two on a rank or file, then one at a right angle. The complete move looks like the capital letter L. It always covers the same distance. It can jump over friendly and enemy units, as if nothing were in the way. Whenever a knight moves, it changes the color of the square it occupies.

THE PAWN: Moves one square straight ahead. Each pawn has the option of advancing two squares on its first move. Captures one square diagonally ahead. Does not capture vertically.

PROMOTION: Pawns reaching the last rank must be changed into a queen, rook, bishop, or knight of the same color. No restrictions (you may have two or more queens).

EN PASSANT: Type of pawn capture. If a pawn is on its fifth rank, and an enemy pawn on an adjacent file advances two squares, the enemy pawn may be captured as if it had advanced only one square. The option may be exercised only on the first opportunity.

CHECK: A direct attack to the king, a threat to capture it next move.

IF "IN CHECK": A king must be taken out of check. It must be moved to safety, the check must be blocked (knight checks can't be blocked), or the checking unit must be captured.

CHECKMATE: When a king can't be taken out of check, the game is over by checkmate. The side giving check wins.

TO CASTLE: To move the king and a rook on the same turn. It must be the first move for both pieces. If the intervening squares are empty, move the king two spaces on the rank toward the rook and move the rook next to the king on the other side.

YOU CAN'T CASTLE: If you are in check or castling into check, or if your king must pass over a square attacked by the enemy (passing through check).

DRAWS: There are five ways to draw: stalemate, agreement, threefold repetition, 50-move rule, and insufficient mating material.

STALEMATE: A player is stalemated if not in check but without a legal move.

AGREEMENT: One player offers a draw, the other accepts.

REPETITION: The player about to repeat the same position for the third time may claim a draw by indicating the intended repetition. The repetition need not be on consecutive moves.

50-MOVE RULE: If 50 moves go by without a capture or pawn move, the player making the 50th move may claim a draw.

INSUFFICIENCY: If neither player has enough material to checkmate, the game is drawn. For example, king vs. king.

EXCHANGE VALUES: A queen is worth about 9, a rook 5, a bishop 3, a knight 3, and a pawn 1.

NOTATION: A way to write down chess moves. Pieces are abbreviated. King = K, queen = Q, rook = R, bishop = B, knight = N, pawn = P (if necessary). In algebraic notation, squares are named by combining a letter (for the file) and a number (for the rank). The files are lettered a–h, starting from White's left. The ranks are numbered 1–8, starting from White's side of the board. White's king starts on e1 and Black's on e8. Some other symbols: check = +, mate = + +, capture = x, kingside castling = 0-0, queenside castling = 0-0-0, good move = !, bad move = ?. If both sides started by moving pawns in front of their kings two squares ahead, the moves are written: 1. e2-e4 e7-e5.

PRINCIPLES AND GUIDELINES

THE CENTER Play for it. Occupy, guard, and influence it. Drive away enemy pieces that control it.

THE INITIATIVE White, having the first move, starts with the initiative. Be aggressive. Don't waste time or moves. Try to attack in ways that build your game. Combine defense with counterattack. Don't be afraid to gambit a pawn for an opening attack, but don't sacrifice without sound reasons. Don't waste time capturing wing pawns at the expense of development.

DEVELOPMENT Use all pieces. Move only center pawns. Aim to develop a different piece on each turn. Move out minor pieces quickly. Castle early. Don't move the same piece repeatedly. Develop with threats.

CASTLING Prepare to castle early in the game, especially if the center is open. Avoid weaknesses in front of the castled king. Castle for both defensive and offensive reasons (to safeguard the king and to activate a rook).

PAWNS Move both center pawns one or two squares ahead, preferably two. Make few pawn moves. Bad pawn moves create weak squares. Don't block center pawns by moving bishops in front of them. Don't move pawns in front of the castled king's position. Trade pawns to avoid loss of material, open lines, or save time.

KNIGHTS Develop knights toward the center, the White ones to f3 and c3, the Black ones to c6 and f6. Develop them elsewhere only if needed or for a particular purpose (e.g. move the KN to h3 to guard f2). Generally move at least one knight before any bishops. Avoid getting knights pinned diagonally by bishops to the king or queen, and on the e-file by rooks to the king.

BISHOPS Place bishops on open diagonals. Use them to guard center squares, pin enemy knights, or defensively to break pins. Flank them if part of a plan to control squares of one color. Avoid unnecessary exchanges for knights. Use them to back up queen and knight attacks.

ROOKS Put rooks on open files (clear of all pawns), half-open files (clear of friendly pawns), or behind advanced friendly pawns. Double them, so that they support each other. Sometimes develop them by moving the pawn in front. Use them to attack the uncastled enemy king along the e-file and to pin enemy units. If feasible, place them on the seventh rank.

THE QUEEN Don't move the queen too early. Don't move it too often. Avoid developing it where it can be attacked. Don't use it if weaker units would suffice. Use it to set up multiple attacks, alone or in combination with other forces. Don't be afraid to trade it for the enemy queen if desirable or to avoid difficulties.

ANALYSIS Evaluate the major elements: material, pawn structure, time, space, and king safety. Elicit information about the position with probing questions. For example: Why did she do that? Did he respond to my last move satisfactorily?

PLANNING Plan early. Don't change plans without good reason. But be flexible. Modify your plan if desirable or necessary. Base your plan on an analysis of the position, noting strengths and weaknesses and accounting for definite threats.

THE ENDGAME Threaten to make new queens by advancing passed pawns. Force your opponent to surrender material trying to stop you. Activate the king. Trade pieces, not pawns, when ahead in material. Position rooks actively behind enemy pawns. Place them on the seventh rank. Don't tie them down to defense. With an extra queen, try to force mate.

D. Tactical Glossary

DISCOVERY: An attack by a stationary piece unveiled when a friendly unit moves out of its way.

DOUBLE THREAT: Two separate threats on the same move but not necessarily given by the same unit.

FORK: An attack by one unit against two different enemy units at the same time.

MATING ATTACK: A general onslaught against the king, resulting in mate or material gain.

MATING NET: A sequence of moves leading to a forced mate.

PIN: An attack on an enemy unit that shields a more valuable unit.

PROMOTION: Moving a pawn to its last rank and changing it into either a queen, rook, bishop, or knight.

REMOVING THE GUARD: Capturing or driving away a unit that guards another.

SKEWER: An attack on an important unit that by moving exposes another unit to capture.

TRAPPING: Winning a unit that has no escape, usually by attacking it with less valuable units.

ZUGZWANG: A situation in which your opponent must move, losing the game or impairing his position.

E. Tactical Maneuvers

(Numbers refer to examples.)

DISCOVERY	42	62	84	85	92
(9)	94	115	159	190	
DOUBLE THREAT	8	15	40	43	91
(10)	117	154	172	177	187
FORK	5	7	12	13	14
(58)	16	17	19	22	24
	26	32	34	35	38
	39	41	44	45	48
	53	55	58	60	61
	63	64	68	69	71
	72	77	80	81	83
	90	95	98	99	103
	106	108	109	111	114
	116	128	130	131	134
	135	148	152	157	158
	178	182	186		
MATING ATTACK	100	175	184		
(3)					
MATING NET	3	27	49	57	74
(26)	75	104	113	121	122
	123	126	127	136	137
	142	145	146	149	150
	160	161	166	167	170
	189				

F. Primary Targets

(Numbers refer to examples.)

a1	1	2				
a2	4	6				
a3	7	8	9	99		
a4	10	11				
a5	16					
a6	17	18				
a7	19	20				
a8	24	106				
b1	3	25	27			
b2	26	28	29			
b3	32	33	51	140		
b4	34	36				
b5	37	38	68			
b6	41	42				
b7	45					
b8	47	48				
c1	49	57	74			
c2	52	77				
c3	56	76				
c4	59	60	103	141		
c5	None					
c6	22	62	64	65	66	71	118
c7	34	46				
c8	None					
d1	78	117				
d2	None					
d3	79	81	187			
d4	31	54	82	83	130	154
d5	67	86				
d6	173					
d7	72	92				
d8	95					

e1	63	97	98	104	127	157	178
	182						
e2	101	102	177				
e3	23	50	105	147			
e4	30	60	107	186			
e5	87	88	89	90	110	111	156
e6	70	112					
e7	131	143					
e8	5	12	14	35	44	58	61
	75	84	109	113	137	155	160
f1	121						
f2	100	124	125	152	158		
f3	73	81	128	129	169		
f4	130	132	153				
f5	133						
f6	116	138					
f7	13	15	21	115	120	139	
f8	119	142					
g1	39	85	114	122	123	126	146
	190						
g2	148	150					
g3	151						
g4	93	172					
g5	159						
g6	162						
g7	91	144	163	164	165		
g8	40	43	80	94	134	135	161
	184	191	192				
h1	96	145	149	170	171	175	
h2	69	108	172	174			
h3	176						
h4	179	180					
h5	181	183					
h6	185						
h7	53	55	187	188			
h8	136	166	167	168	189		

G. Secondary Targets

(Numbers refer to examples.)

a1	18	77	99			
a2	5					
a3	None					
a4	12					
a5	13	14	15	41	94	
a6	16					
a7	21					
a8	17	22	23	37	40	64	134
b1	None					
b2	30					
b3	31					
b4	35					
b5	12	39				
b6	116					
b7	43	44	135			
b8	46					
c1	50	51	132			
c2	38	53	54	56		
c3	9	26	30	55	103	
c4	58	111	128			
c5	48	61	62	63		
c6	16	87				
c7	8	67	68	69		
c8	52	70	72	95		
d1	73					
d2	180					
d3	10	80				
d4	84	147				
d5	24	85	159			
d6	68	90				
d7	91	112				
d8	88	96				

e1	7	26	78	83	99	100	105
	111	152	186				
e2	54	129					
e3	103						
e4	76	106	108	158			
e5	92	109					
e6	114						
e7	117						
e8	17	22	41	64	65	89	93
	101	107	118	120	162		
f1	59	79	129				
f2	133	151					
f3	38	98	102	177			
f4	131						
f5	72	187					
f6	90	184					
f7	88	140	141	148			
f8	36	124	143	144			
g1	19	82	98	125	147	163	177
g2	45	176					
g3	152						
g4	115	154	155	156			
g5	157	158					
g6	None						
g7	42	168					
g8	24	32	71	95	164		
h1	45	169					
h2	173						
h3	33	148					
h4	178						
h5	92	182					
h6	186						
h7	None						
h8	110	190	192				

Index

238

About the Author

Bruce Pandolfini is the author of sixteen instructional chess books, including *More Chess Openings: Traps and Zaps 2; Beginning Chess; Pandolfini's Chess Complete; Chessercizes; More Chessercizes; Checkmate; Principles of the New Chess; Pandolfini's Endgame Course; Russian Chess; The ABC's of Chess; Let's Play Chess; Kasparov's Winning Chess Tactics; One-Move Chess by the Champions; Chess Openings: Traps and Zaps; Square One;* and *Weapons of Chess.* He is also the editor of the distinguished anthologies *The Best of Chess Life & Review,* Volumes I and II, and has produced, with David MacEnulty, two instructional videotapes, *Understanding Chess* and *Opening Principles.*

Bruce was the chief commentator at the New York half of the 1990 Kasparov–Karpov World Chess Championship and in 1990, was head coach of the United States Team in the World Youth Chess Championships in Wisconsin. Perhaps the most experienced chess teacher in North America, he is co-founder, with Faneuil Adams, of the Manhattan Chess Club School and is the director of the New York City Schools Program. Bruce's most famous student, six-time National Scholastic Champion Joshua Waitzkin, is the subject of Fred Waitzkin's acclaimed book *Searching for Bobby Fischer* and of the movie of the same name. Bruce Pandolfini lives in New York City.